THE 100 MOST ASKED QUESTIONS ABOUT ANGELS, DEMONS, AND THE SUPERNATURAL

Books by S. Michael Houdmann

The 100 Most Asked Questions About God and the Bible

The 100 Most Asked Questions About Heaven, Hell, and the Afterlife

The 100 Most Asked Questions About Angels, Demons, and the Supernatural

THE 100 MOST ASKED QUESTIONS ABOUT ANGELS, DEMONS, AND THE SUPERNATURAL

• • •

Scripture's Answers on Spiritual Warfare and More

S. Michael Houdmann

BETHANYHOUSE
a division of Baker Publishing Group
Minneapolis, Minnesota

Published by Bethany House Publishers
Minneapolis, Minnesota
BethanyHouse.com

Bethany House Publishers is a division of
Baker Publishing Group, Grand Rapids, Michigan

Printed in the United States of America

Library of Congress Cataloging-in-Publication Data
Names: Houdmann, S. Michael author
Title: The 100 most asked questions about angels, demons, and the supernatural : scripture's answers on spiritual warfare and more / S. Michael Houdmann.
Other titles: One hundred most asked questions about angels, demons, and the supernatural
Description: Minneapolis, Minnesota : Bethany House, a division of Baker Publishing Group, [2026]
Identifiers: LCCN 2026021479 | ISBN 9780764245800 paperback | ISBN 9781493455393 ebook
Subjects: LCSH: Angels—Biblical teaching | Devil—Biblical teaching | Spiritual warfare—Biblical teaching
Classification: LCC BS680.A48 H68 2026
LC record available at https://lccn.loc.gov/2026021479

Baker Publishing Group publications use paper produced from sustainable forestry practices and postconsumer waste whenever possible.

26 27 28 29 30 31 32 7 6 5 4 3 2 1

Contents

Introduction

Little did I know what God had in mind when I launched Got Questions.org over twenty-four years ago. What my wife and I thought would be a fun hobby turned out to be something God intended to expand into one of the most impactful Christian websites in the world. Now, not only do I have my dream job, but I also get to watch God take our limited vision and use it in ways far beyond anything we could ask or imagine.

GotQuestions.org has received over a million personally submitted questions from around the world. Each month, the articles on GotQuestions.org are read approximately twenty million times. Over the years, our articles have been read over 2.6 billion times. These interactions give GotQuestions.org plenty of data regarding what questions people are truly asking. We *know* what people are asking. We *know* the information people are searching for. And, after years of God refining us and the content we produce, we have improved at answering questions in an understandable and applicable way.

This book contains the top one hundred questions we have received related to angels, demons, Satan, the supernatural, and spiritual warfare. Many of the questions are of vital importance.

Some of the questions are immensely personal. A few of the questions are fairly obscure. None of the questions are trivial.

My sincerest hope is that you will find this resource interesting, informative, biblically accurate, and worth sharing with others. My utmost desire would be that you would come to an understanding of what God's Word says about the spiritual realm: our allies, our enemies, and how to engage with them. May this book motivate you to continue asking questions and continue looking to God's Word for the answers.

—S. Michael Houdmann

SECTION 1

Questions About the Spiritual Realm

1. What are spiritual beings?

A spiritual being is a supernatural, incorporeal being. The Bible begins with the assertion that God, a spiritual being, created the heavens and the earth (Genesis 1:1). Other spiritual beings mentioned in Scripture include angels, demons, and Satan. The supernatural worldview is found throughout the Bible—from creation to Revelation and everywhere in between. While we may never fully understand everything that has to do with spiritual beings this side of heaven, believers worship God, who is spirit (John 4:24), and look forward to His kingdom, which is not of this world (John 18:36).

God is a spiritual being. God has no physical form, and nothing in this world can be made to represent Him (Exodus 20:4; Deuteronomy 4:12; Acts 17:29). There are other spiritual beings who are not of the same status, greatness, or ability as God. The psalmist declares,

> The heavens praise your wonders, LORD, your faithfulness too, in the assembly of the holy ones. For who in the skies above can compare with the LORD? Who is like the LORD among the heavenly beings? In the council of the holy ones God is greatly feared; he is more awesome than all who surround him. Who is like you, LORD God Almighty? You, LORD, are mighty, and your faithfulness surrounds you."
>
> Psalm 89:5–8

In just this section of Scripture, we are made aware of an assembly of holy ones, heavenly beings, and the Lord God Almighty who is greater than all other spiritual beings.

God created the spiritual beings. They are known as God's heavenly host (Psalm 148:2; Luke 2:13). When God laid the foundation of the earth, "the morning stars sang together and all the angels shouted for joy" (Job 38:7). These spiritual beings existed before God made humanity.

If a being is "spiritual," that being is not a human or an animal—both human beings and animals exist with a physical body. The term *spiritual being* does not tell us what the being does. Angels, for example, are spiritual beings (Psalm 104:4). Yet the term *angels* can be used for several different types of spiritual beings. Angels exist within a hierarchy and have various functions. Some angels are loyal to God, and others, the fallen angels, are loyal to the devil (Matthew 25:41). Messenger angels (Luke 1:26–31; 2:10–11; Matthew 1:20), archangels (1 Thessalonians 4:16; Jude 1:9), cherubim (Genesis 3:24), seraphim (Isaiah 6:2), watchers (Daniel 4:13, 17, 23), and the divine council (Jeremiah 23:18) all seem to be part of God's heavenly host.

Besides the holy members of the heavenly host, there are other spiritual beings who form the powers of darkness (Ephesians 6:12).

These rulers, authorities, powers of this dark world, and spiritual forces of evil also reside in the heavenly realms. The wicked spiritual beings include "demons" (Mark 1:34) or "impure spirits" (Luke 4:36), false gods and goddesses (Exodus 15:11; Deuteronomy 11:16; 32:17), and renegade "sons of God" (Genesis 6:2, 4). These are all spiritual beings, but their loyalty is not to the Lord of hosts. Our battle in this world is not against flesh and blood but against these spiritual forces in the heavenly realms (Ephesians 6:12).

The devil is also a spiritual being who aspired to promote himself above God (Isaiah 14:12–15). His pride led to his fall, and he continues in his wickedness. Although the devil is referred to as "the ruler of this world" (John 12:31 ESV; cf. 2 Corinthians 4:4), his power is not equal to God's. The devil can only do what God allows. His demise is sure, along with that of all the demons who follow him (Matthew 25:41; Revelation 20:3).

We cannot see the spiritual realm, and we would never be able to see God, except for the Incarnation. The Son of God, the Word who always was God (John 1:1), took on human flesh and dwelt among us (v. 14). Jesus Christ is the "the image of the invisible God, the firstborn over all creation. For in him all things were created: things in heaven and on earth, visible and invisible, whether thrones or powers or rulers or authorities; all things have been created through him and for him" (Colossians 1:15–16). Jesus, God in the flesh, lived a perfect life, and His perfect sacrifice on the cross provided our redemption once and for all (Hebrews 7:27; 9:12, 28; 10:10). In addition to reconciling us to God, the sacrifice of Christ also "disarmed the powers and authorities" of the spiritual realm (Colossians 2:15).

Among all the spiritual beings, there is no one like our God. There is none greater. No other spiritual being is worthy of our worship.

At the end of our lives, we will enter a spiritual realm. Believers in Christ are carried by angels to the place where the Lord is (see Luke 16:22). Unbelievers will face eternity in hell, separated from God. For believers, faith will become sight.

2. What are the heavenly hosts?

On the night that Jesus was born, an angel announced the good news to the shepherds in the fields of Bethlehem. "Suddenly a great company of the heavenly host appeared with the angel" and joined in praise to God (Luke 2:13). Most hymnals include "Praise God from Whom All Blessings Flow" (also known as "The Doxology"), one of the great hymns of the faith, and that song includes the line "Praise Him above, ye heav'nly host."[1] In both of these contexts, the heavenly hosts are God's holy angels who dwell in God's presence.

Basically, the word *host* refers to a great number of individuals or to an army. Modified by the word *heavenly*, *hosts* becomes a great number of angelic beings forming a celestial army under God's command. There is a suggestion of rank and orderliness, of companies and divisions within that heavenly army. The heavenly hosts were created by God and are controlled by God.

One of God's names is "Lord of hosts," which occurs often in the Old Testament. In Hebrew, it is *Yahweh Sabaoth*, meaning "Lord of the heavenly armies" or "God of the heavenly hosts." The NIV translates the name as "Lord Almighty" (see 1 Samuel 1:3; Psalm 24:10; Isaiah 22:14; Jeremiah 2:19; Haggai 2:9; Zechariah 8:6; Malachi 2:16).

There are places in Scripture where the heavenly hosts include fallen angels, such as in 1 Kings 22:19. The prophet Micaiah relates a vision of God's throne room, where he saw "the whole heavenly host" standing on God's right and left (HCSB). One of these beings in the divine presence is a "deceiving spirit" (v. 22), so the term *heavenly hosts* can refer broadly to all angelic beings, holy and unholy.

Psalm 148:2 equates the parallel terms *angels* and *heavenly hosts*: "Praise him, all his angels; praise him, all his heavenly hosts." Psalm 103:19–21 gives further information: "The Lord has established his throne in heaven, and his kingdom rules over all. Praise the Lord, you his angels, you mighty ones who do his bidding, who obey his word. Praise the LORD, all his heavenly hosts, you his servants who do his will." In this passage, the psalmist praises God for the extent of divine authority—there is no part of creation that is not under God's rule; His throne is "established." The heavenly hosts (the angels) praise the Lord; they are, in fact, God's servants who are at His beck and call. They dutifully obey God's commands, carry out His bidding, and acquiesce to His will.

As believers, we will someday inhabit heaven with God and the heavenly hosts. According to Hebrews 12:22, we have been called to the place where there dwell "thousands upon thousands of angels in joyful assembly." When Jesus returns to earth to establish His kingdom, "the armies of heaven [will be] following him, riding on white horses and dressed in fine linen, white and clean" (Revelation 19:14). In this context, the heavenly hosts are all those who inhabit heaven at that time: the redeemed of the church age, Old Testament believers, martyrs of the tribulation, and angels. The angelic army will be augmented by humans redeemed by the blood of the Lamb. We will not become angels, but we will be with them in glory.

3. What is the divine council?

Psalm 89:5–7 says, "The heavens praise your wonders, LORD, your faithfulness too, in the assembly of the holy ones. For who in the skies above can compare with the LORD? Who is like the LORD among the heavenly beings? In the council of the holy ones God is greatly feared; he is more awesome than all who surround him." These verses present a divine council: heavenly beings referred to as "the council of the holy ones." Psalm 82:1 (ESV) also indicates that "God has taken his place in the divine council." The "divine council" is also called the "great assembly" (NIV), "heaven's court" (NLT), and "His own congregation" (NASB1995). This divine council could also be referenced in Nehemiah 9:6, which says, "You alone are the LORD; You have made heaven, the heaven of heavens, with all their host, the earth and everything on it, the seas and all that is in them, and You preserve them all. The host of heaven worships You" (NKJV). The "host" of the "heaven of heavens" are most likely angelic beings. God is the Lord of hosts (Psalm 24:10; Isaiah 44:6). The God who presides in the heavenly council is sovereign over all, including the spiritual beings in His divine council.

Other passages of Scripture describe scenes that could be interpreted as a meeting of the divine council. In Job 1:6, a conclave is held in heaven: "One day the angels came to present themselves before the LORD." In 1 Kings 22:19, the prophet Micaiah relates a vision: "I saw the LORD sitting on his throne with all the multitudes of heaven standing around him on his right and on his left." Micaiah goes on to describe how the spiritual beings there suggested various means of accomplishing God's will, and God chose one spirit to carry out the task. In Daniel 4:17, the angels present a decision made by the divine council: "This decision is by the decree of the watchers, and the sentence by the word of the holy ones, in order that the living may know that the Most High rules in the kingdom of men, gives it to whomever He will, and sets over it the lowest of men" (NKJV). The divine council in God's presence was given the task of deciding Nebuchadnezzar's judgment and communicating the verdict to Daniel in a dream.

God does not need a divine council to give Him ideas or to approve His decisions. He is the omniscient God Almighty. However, in His wisdom, God has created a divine council to stand in His presence, and He graciously allows them to participate in various judgments and decrees.

It is a wonder that God allows created beings to be privy to His ways and even have input in His plan. The divine council is privileged to participate in God's plans, and, to an extent, so are we: "The prayer of a righteous person is powerful and effective" (James 5:16). And God chooses to use us as ministers of reconciliation in the sharing of the gospel: "Therefore go and make disciples of all nations, baptizing them in the name of the Father and of the Son and of the Holy Spirit" (Matthew 28:19; cf. 2 Corinthians 5:18).

4. What evidence is there of a spiritual realm?

The Bible teaches the existence of an immaterial, spiritual reality, unseen by human eyes. The physical reality is evident for all to see—although some doubt the existence of a material universe, too! The Bible says that the spiritual realm consists of both good—God and the holy angels—and evil—the devil and his demons. Demons are most likely fallen angels who rebelled against God and lost their position in heaven (see Ezekiel 28:11–17; Isaiah 14:12–15; Revelation 12:7–9). The Bible also teaches that humans were created by God in His image, which means we have a spiritual component (Genesis 1:27). We are more than physical entities; we possess a soul/spirit destined for eternity. Even though the spiritual realm is invisible to the physical eye, we are connected to it, and what goes on in the spiritual realm directly affects our physical world.

In our culture, the most commonly accepted form of evidence for proving the existence of something is empirical evidence, which involves using the scientific method of observation and experimentation. Is there empirical evidence for a spiritual realm? Unsurprisingly, there is "evidence" both for and against the existence of a spiritual realm. It comes down to which studies one wants to believe.

The best and most prevalent evidence available to prove there is a spiritual realm is testimonial evidence. Consider the sheer number of religions around the world and the billions of people who focus their lives on the spiritual realm: Is it likely that so many people are mistaken about their encounters with the spiritual realm?

The best testimonial evidence for a spiritual realm is the Bible itself. Historians, both Christian and non-Christian, agree that the historical authenticity of the Bible is strong. Jesus claimed to be God's Son, the One who came down from heaven: "You are from below; I am from above. You are of this world; I am not of this world" (John 8:23). The Bible relates numerous encounters between people and the spiritual realm. Jesus cast demons out of people regularly, healed the sick with a word, miraculously fed thousands, and spoke with Moses and Elijah in person (Matthew 17:1–3). These are all indicators that the spiritual realm is real.

5. What does it mean that we do not fight against flesh and blood (Ephesians 6:12)?

In Ephesians 6:12, the apostle Paul introduces the believers in Ephesus to the reality of spiritual warfare in the Christian life: "For we are not fighting against flesh-and-blood enemies, but against evil rulers and authorities of the unseen world, against mighty powers in this dark world, and against evil spirits in the heavenly places" (Ephesians 6:12 NLT). Before discussing the armor Christians must wear in combat and their weapons of warfare, Paul stresses that the battle is spiritual, not physical. *We do not fight against flesh and blood* means that we do not face a physical enemy but a spiritual one.

Christian warfare consists of a spiritual strategy fought with supernatural weapons against an unseen enemy. The opposition is real but not visible to the naked eye. Beneath the surface, an invisible spiritual battle is raging. We fight this war not with tangible weapons like guns and ammunition, nor with bodily defenses such as kicks and punches, but by daily putting on the whole armor of God, always praying, standing firm in the Word of God, and staying alert (Ephesians 6:13–18).

If we do not fight against flesh and blood, whom are we wrestling with, and who are our spiritual enemies? Paul named these opponents as the devil and his schemes, the rulers, authorities, and "powers of this dark world," and "the spiritual forces of evil in the heavenly realms" (Ephesians 6:12). His description seems to indicate a pecking order of evil beings who do Satan's bidding to oppose God's will on earth.

The apostle Peter also warned believers to remain vigilant against the devil: "Be alert and of sober mind. Your enemy the devil prowls around like a roaring lion looking for someone to devour. Resist him, standing firm in the faith" (1 Peter 5:8–9).

The Bible calls the devil, or Satan, "the prince of this world" (John 12:31), "the ruler of the kingdom of the air, the spirit who is now at work in those who are disobedient" (Ephesians 2:2), "the god of this age" (2 Corinthians 4:4), and "the accuser" of believers (Revelation 12:10). This is our true enemy.

Paul says, in our fight with this enemy, we must be aware of his tactics (2 Corinthians 2:11). And in Ephesians 6:11–12, Paul mentions three main traits of Satan's spiritual forces. First, they are powerful. They have authority to rule in the world. Second, they are evil. These wicked spiritual enemies use their power to wreak destruction. They are associated with darkness and not light, wickedness and not good. And third, they are shrewd. They know how to scheme and strategize. They are so skilled at deception that sometimes they come disguised as angels of light (2 Corinthians 11:14) or wolves in sheep's clothing (Matthew 7:15).

So how can we, in our human weakness, expect to stand against such strong and cunning enemies? Brute strength won't win the battle. Humanly speaking, victory is impossible. In our struggle against the devil and his scheming forces, Paul says we must "be strong in the Lord and in his mighty power" (Ephesians 6:10). It is our job to stand aside and let God fight the battle for us, and only then are we sure to win.

Only God can strengthen, defend, and deliver us from the power, wickedness, and craft of the devil (2 Timothy 4:17–18). Our enemy may be strong, but God is stronger (1 John 4:4). God makes available to us the same mighty power that raised Jesus

Christ from the dead and seated Him at God's right hand in heaven (Ephesians 1:19–20). Our enemies are defeated through Christ's victory over them on the cross (Colossians 2:15).

When David came up against the Philistine giant, he recognized that his fight was not ultimately against flesh and blood. Goliath taunted David and cursed his God, saying, "Am I a dog, that you come at me with sticks? . . . Come here . . . and I'll give your flesh to the birds and the wild animals!" (1 Samuel 17:43–44). But David, trusting in the strength of the Lord and His mighty power, answered, "You come against me with sword and spear and javelin, but I come against you in the name of the LORD Almighty, the God of the armies of Israel, whom you have defied" (1 Samuel 17:45).

"For the battle is the LORD's," declared David (1 Samuel 17:47), and so ought we as we engage in spiritual warfare. Our fight is not against flesh and blood. The victory depends on the Lord, not us.

SECTION 2

Questions About the Origin and Purpose of Angels

6. Do angels appear to people today?

In the Bible angels appear to people in unpredictable and various ways. From a casual reading of Scripture, a person might get the idea that angelic appearances were somewhat common, but that is not the case. There is an increasing interest in angels today, and there are many reports of angelic appearances. Angels are part of almost every religion and generally seem to have the same role of messenger. In order to determine whether angels appear today, we must first get a biblical view of their ancient appearances.

The first appearance of angels in the Bible is in Genesis 3:24, when Adam and Eve were expelled from the Garden of Eden. God placed cherubim to block the entrance with a flaming sword. The next angelic appearance is in Genesis 16:7, about 1,900 years later. Hagar, the Egyptian servant who bore Ishmael to Abraham, was instructed by an angel to return and submit to her mistress, Sarai. Abraham was visited by God and two angels in Genesis 18:2, when God informed him of the impending destruction of Sodom and Gomorrah. The same two angels visited Lot and instructed him to escape the city with his family before it was destroyed (Genesis 19:1–11). The angels in this case also displayed supernatural power by blinding the wicked men who were threatening Lot.

When Jacob saw a multitude of angels (Genesis 32:1), he immediately recognized them as the army of God. In Numbers 22:22, an angel confronted the disobedient prophet Balaam, but Balaam did not see the angel at first, although his donkey did. Mary received a visit from an angel who told her that she would be the mother of the Messiah, and Joseph was warned by an angel to take Mary and Jesus to Egypt to protect them from Herod's edict (Matthew 2:13). When angels appear, those who see them are often struck with fear (Judges 6:22; 1 Chronicles 21:30; Matthew 28:5). Angels deliver messages from God and do His bidding, sometimes by supernatural means. In every case, the angels point people to God and give the glory to Him. Holy angels refuse to be worshiped (Revelation 22:8–9).

According to modern reports, angelic visitations come in a variety of forms. In some cases, a stranger prevents serious injury or death and then mysteriously disappears. In other cases, a winged or white-clothed being is seen momentarily and is then gone. The person who sees the angel is often left with a feeling of peace and assurance of God's presence. This type of visitation seems to agree with the biblical pattern as seen in Acts 27:23–24.

Another type of visitation that is sometimes reported today is the "angel choir" type. In Luke 2:13, the shepherds were visited by a heavenly choir as they were told of the birth of Jesus. Some people have reported similar experiences in places of worship. This experience does not fit the model so well, as it typically serves no purpose other than to provide a feeling of spiritual elation. The angel choir in Luke's Gospel was heralding some very specific news.

A third type of visitation involves only a physical feeling. Elderly people have often reported feeling as though arms or wings were wrapped around them in times of extreme loneliness. God is certainly the God of all comfort, and Scripture speaks of God covering us with His wings (Psalm 91:4). Such reports may be examples of that covering.

God is still as active in the world as He has always been, and His angels are certainly still at work. Just as angels protected God's people in the past, we can be assured that they are guarding us today. Hebrews 13:2 says, "Be not forgetful to entertain strangers: for thereby some have entertained angels unawares" (KJV). As we obey God's commands, it is quite possible that we may encounter His angels, even if we do not realize it. In special circumstances, God allowed His people to see His unseen angels, so God's people would be encouraged and continue in His service (2 Kings 6:16–17).

We must also heed the warnings of Scripture concerning angelic beings: There are fallen angels who work for Satan who will do anything to subvert and destroy us. Galatians 1:8 warns us to beware of any "new" gospel, even if it is delivered by an angel. Colossians 2:18 warns against the worship of angels. Every time in the Bible when men bowed down before holy angels, those beings firmly refused to be worshiped. Any angel who receives worship or who does not give glory to the Lord Jesus is an imposter. Second Corinthians 11:14–15 states that Satan and his angels disguise themselves as angels of light in order to deceive and lead astray.

We are encouraged by the knowledge that God's angels are at work. In special circumstances, we might even have one of those rare personal visitations. Greater than that knowledge, however, is the knowledge that Jesus Himself has said, "Surely I am with you always, even to the very end of the age" (Matthew 28:20). Jesus, who made the angels and receives their worship, has promised us His own presence in our trials.

7. Do angels exist?

The Bible speaks of angels as real, actual beings. However, Scripture's depiction of angels is very different from the popular concept of them. The Bible describes angels as vastly powerful, intimidating, and mysterious creatures. They serve God in specific tasks and are not wandering or random creatures. While we don't have a great deal of information about angels in the Bible, what's available is enough to correct some common misconceptions.

The word *angel* comes from the Greek word *aggelos* (or *angelos*), which most literally means "messenger." In Old Testament Hebrew, these beings are called *mal'ak*, which means the same thing, "messenger." Communication seems to be the primary function of angels in the Bible. Most references to angels involve their delivering some news or command on behalf of God. They are occasionally depicted as protecting certain people (Daniel 6:20–23) or nations (Daniel 12:1). However, there is no direct biblical support for the concept of a "guardian angel"—a single spiritual entity assigned to a specific person for purposes of protection or guidance—although such beings may exist.

In modern times, common depictions of angels include things like halos, feathery wings, flowing hair, harps, and white robes—or sometimes they're portrayed as chubby infants with tiny wings and shining eyes. In reality, the Bible gives no general visual description of angels. We have a few details concerning the appearance of cherubim and seraphim (Isaiah 6:2–6; Ezekiel 1:4–28). Some angels, such as those at the ascension, are described as wearing white (Acts 1:10). Scripture indicates that angels can take on a mundane human form (Genesis 19:1–4).

Most people in Scripture who encounter angels react with fear. Almost every time an angel appears to someone, the angel's first words are, "Don't be afraid" (Luke 1:13, 30; 2:10; Matthew 28:5). Their presence can be so overwhelming that even the most God-fearing men had to be warned not to worship them (Revelation 19:9–10). As spiritual beings created to serve God, angels are not so much "cute" as they are powerful, awe-inspiring, and otherworldly.

Yes, angels are real. The cartoonish versions of angels so often seen in movies and commercials do nothing to aid our understanding.

8. When did God create the angels?

Trying to determine when God created the angels is tricky because anything God did before the foundation of the world puts the event outside of time itself. Time and space are characteristics of our created world, not God's uncreated existence. He is not limited by hours, days, and years as we are. In fact, the Bible tells us that "with the Lord a day is like a thousand years, and a thousand years are like a day" (2 Peter 3:8).

We do know that God created the angels before He created the physical universe. The book of Job describes the angels worshiping God as He was creating the world. God asks, "Where were you when I laid the foundations of the earth? Tell Me, if you have understanding. Who determined its measurements? . . . Or who laid its cornerstone, when the morning stars sang together, and all the sons of God shouted for joy?" (Job 38:4–7 NKJV). In this passage, the "morning stars" and "sons of God" are references to angels.

If we consider the function of angels, we might conclude that God created the angels just prior to the creation of mankind because one of their duties is to be "ministering spirits sent to serve those who will inherit salvation" (Hebrews 1:14). We also know that angels existed prior to the Garden of Eden, because Satan, who was formerly the angel Lucifer, was already present in the garden in his fallen state. However, because another function of angels is to worship God around His throne (Revelation 5:11–14), they may have been in existence millions of years—as we reckon time—before God created the world, worshiping Him and serving Him.

So, we don't know specifically when God created the angels. It was sometime before the world was created. Whether this was a day before, or billions of years before—again, as we reckon time—we cannot be sure.

9. Why did God allow Satan and the demons to sin?

To both the angels and humanity, God gave a will, and He allowed them to make a choice. While the Bible does not give many details regarding the rebellion of Satan and the fallen angels, it seems that Lucifer—probably the greatest of all the angels (Ezekiel 28:12–18)—in pride chose to rebel against God in order to seek to become his own god. Satan (as Lucifer is now known) did not want to worship or obey God; he wanted to be God (Isaiah 14:12–14). Revelation 12:4 is a figurative description of one third of the angels choosing to follow Satan in his rebellion, becoming the fallen angels—demons.

Unlike the choice facing humanity, however, the choice the angels had (to follow Satan or remain faithful to God) seems to have been eternally binding. The Bible hints at no opportunity for the fallen angels to repent and be forgiven. Jesus died for the salvation of humanity, not of angels (Hebrews 2:16). Nor does the Bible indicate that it is possible for more of the angels to sin.

The angels who remain faithful to God are described as the "elect angels" (1 Timothy 5:21). Satan and the fallen angels knew God in all His glory. For them to rebel, despite what they knew about God, was the utmost evil, and God does not give them the opportunity to repent. Further, the Bible gives us no reason to believe they *would* repent even if God gave them the chance. God gave Satan and the angels the same choice He gave Adam and Eve, to obey Him or not. The angels had a freewill choice to make; God did not force or encourage any of the angels to sin. Satan and the fallen angels sinned on their own and will one day face God's eternal wrath in the lake of fire.

Why did God give the angels this choice, when He knew what the results would be? God knew that one third of the angels would rebel and therefore be cursed to eternal fire. God also knew that Satan would further his rebellion by tempting humanity into sin. So, why did God allow it? The Bible does not explicitly give the answer to this question. Ultimately, it comes back to God's sovereignty over His creation. The psalmist says, "As for God, his way is perfect" (Psalm 18:30). Since God's ways are "perfect," we can trust whatever He does and accept whatever He allows. So, the perfect plan from our perfect God was to allow sin. Our minds are not God's mind, nor are our ways His ways, as He reminds us in Isaiah 55:8–9.

10. Are the holy angels perfect, or do they sometimes fail God?

Scripture contains many stories of angels doing God's work. Angels are assigned to protecting believers (Psalm 91:11; Matthew 4:6), carrying messages to humankind (Matthew 1:20; Luke 1:26–28; Daniel 9:20–23), and helping judge the earth (Matthew 13:39–49). Angels praise God and intercede for believers (Psalm 148:2; Matthew 18:10), but they are not omniscient (Matthew 24:36).

They are described as mighty beings who do God's bidding and obey His word (Psalm 103:20). We know that God is perfect (Matthew 5:48) and that nothing imperfect can dwell in His presence. Since we know that angels do dwell in His presence (Matthew 18:10), we can assume that the holy angels are indeed perfect. Jesus calls them "holy angels" for a reason (Luke 9:26).

There are two passages in Job that seem to contradict the idea of angels being perfect. The first is Job 4:18, and the second is Job 15:15. These two verses are part of two separate speeches by Job's friend Eliphaz, who is attempting to help Job make sense of his misfortunes. Job was a righteous man who feared God and lived blamelessly (Job 1:1). Therefore, the multiple tragedies he suffered seemed very odd to the minds of his religious friends, for they reasoned that God rewards the good with pleasurable things and the evil with painful things. From that wrong premise, they told Job that his pain and tragedy were the result of sin in his life. When Job maintained his innocence, his friends doubted him.

Eliphaz then steps forward and argues against Job's innocence, using angels as proof: "If God . . . charges his angels with error, how much more those who live in houses of clay?" (Job 4:18–19). In other words, if even the angels are faulted before God, certainly human beings are incapable of living innocently! In another speech to Job, Eliphaz returns to the same theme: "If God places no trust in his holy ones, if even the heavens are not pure in his eyes, how much less mortals, who are vile and corrupt . . . ?" (Job 15:15–16).

There are two things that we must keep in mind. First, Eliphaz was not a truth-teller. In fact, at the end of the book of Job, when the Lord Himself appears, we read this: "[God] said to Eliphaz the Temanite, 'I am angry with you and your two friends, because you have not spoken the truth about me'" (Job 42:7). Thus, it is important to always know who is speaking in the book of Job. The words of Eliphaz and the other two of Job's friends are unreliable.

Second, in the verses previous to Job 4:18, we see that Eliphaz got his information from a spirit that had visited him in the night (Job 4:12–16). This spirit did not appear to Eliphaz the way the holy angels appeared to Daniel, Mary, or Joseph. The holy angels came in the light, announced that their messages were from God, and told the humans they visited not to fear. The spirit that appeared to Eliphaz, on the other hand, frightened him, hid in the darkness, and whispered in his ear. It is certain that the spirit that appeared to Eliphaz was a demon, a fallen angel who was expressing its own bitterness at being charged with error by a holy God.

These two passages in Job, though they at first glance may appear to contradict the idea of holy angels, do not prove the imperfection of God's angels. Instead, they prove the imperfection of man, who is easily deceived and must always ask God for wisdom instead of relying on his own susceptible intellect (see Proverbs 3:5–6; James 1:5).

11. Is it possible that more of the angels could sin?

First Timothy 5:21 says, "I charge you, in the sight of God and Christ Jesus and the elect angels, to keep these instructions without partiality, and to do nothing out of favoritism." No matter what view one takes on election, the Bible is clear that God was somehow involved in choosing who would be saved—or, in this case, which of the angels would not sin.

God is sovereign in all His choices: He chose Abraham to be the father of many nations (Genesis 17:4–5); He chose Israel to be His special people (Genesis 17:7); He chose Mary to be the mother of Jesus (Luke 1:35–37); He chose the twelve apostles to live with the Lord Jesus for three years and learn from Him (Mark 3:13–19); and He chose Paul to bring the gospel to many people (Acts 9:1–19). In the same way, He has chosen people "from every tribe and language and people and nation" (Revelation 5:9) to come to faith in Christ. Those whom He has chosen will come to Him, and He will never cast them out.

It seems that God also made a choice concerning the angels. God's holy angels are "elect," meaning that God has chosen them. Perhaps God gave all the angels a onetime choice to obey Him or not. Those who sinned and followed Lucifer are condemned, never to be redeemed. Those who chose to remain loyal to God are called "elect" and are confirmed in holiness. The Bible gives no reason to believe that more of the angels could sin; it does not seem possible that the holy angels could lose their "elect" status.

12. What is the purpose of angels?

When we think of angels, images that come to mind may include naked cherubs, wings, halos, and cute kindergartners in the Christmas play. But God's Word doesn't spend much time describing what angels look like. It's clearer on the purpose of angels: Hebrews 1:7 says, "He makes his angels spirits, and his servants flames of fire."

Scripture gives us only glimpses into the supernatural realm, but those glimpses are enough to learn that angels perform a variety of tasks:

1. *Angels serve the people God saves.* One purpose of angels is to minister to the elect of God: "Are not all angels ministering spirits sent to serve those who will inherit salvation?" (Hebrews 1:14). Paul experienced an angelic visitation during a storm at sea. The angel brought him comfort (Acts 27:23–24). Others who have been served by angels include Elijah (1 Kings 19:3–8) and Peter (Acts 12:6–10).
2. *Angels deliver messages.* The word *angel* literally means "messenger." In the Bible, angels usually appeared as human men when they delivered messages from God to

people (see Genesis 18:1–3). The angel Gabriel appeared to at least three people in the Bible. He interpreted a vision for Daniel (Daniel 8:16), told Zechariah about the birth of John the Baptist (Luke 1:19), and proclaimed to Mary that she would be the mother of the Messiah (Luke 1:26). Angels in the form of men also warned Lot of God's impending judgment on Sodom and Gomorrah (Genesis 19:1).

3. *Angels wage spiritual battle.* Another purpose of angels is to fight the forces of spiritual darkness (Ephesians 6:12; Jude 1:9). When an angel appeared to Daniel to deliver the interpretation of a vision, the angel stated that Michael the archangel had to help him fight his way through enemy forces (Daniel 10:10–14). Angelic warfare is also mentioned in Revelation 12:7. The full extent of this warfare is not known to us, but it would seem that a fierce cosmic battle rages just out of sight.
4. *Angels worship God.* Angels constantly surround the throne of God, worshiping Him and shouting His praises (Psalm 148:1–2; Isaiah 6:3; Hebrews 1:6; Revelation 5:8–13). Angels were created to worship God, and some rejected that purpose, committing an unforgivable wrong. When Lucifer, a chief angel, refused to worship God and insisted that angels worship him instead, God removed him from his position in heaven (Isaiah 14:12–18). The angels siding with Lucifer were exiled with him.
5. *Angels serve.* Angels exist to do the will of their Creator. They go where God sends them, say what He gives them to say, and minister to His children on earth (Psalm 103:20; Revelation 22:9; Hebrews 1:14). After Jesus' forty-day temptation in the wilderness, angels came and ministered to Him (Matthew 4:11). When the righteous die, it seems that angels carry them straight to the place of God's rest (Luke 16:22).

6. *Angels execute judgment.* Angels are not all joy and glad tidings. They also carry out God's orders for destruction. The book of Revelation foretells the involvement of angels in many events that will bring about the ultimate destruction of the world (Revelation 7:1; 8–10). When Pharaoh refused to let the people of God leave Egypt, God sent an angel to strike down every firstborn son (Exodus 12:12, 23). Angels were involved in the death of Herod (Acts 12:23), the slaughter of the Assyrian army (2 Kings 19:35), and the punishment of Jerusalem (1 Chronicles 21:15).
7. *Angels aided in the transmission of God's Word.* Hebrews 2:2 describes the Mosaic Law as "the message spoken through angels." In some way, angels were involved in the process of Moses receiving the law on Sinai.

God uses angels in many ways. Because there is so much we do not know about the world outside our physical universe, we cannot possibly understand all the purposes angels fulfill. But Christians have the confidence that God's holy angels stand ready to protect and deliver God's mortal children (Psalm 91:11). Angels are created beings, as we are, and should never be worshiped, but we can thank the Lord for them and the unseen ways He uses them to impact our lives.

13. What does it mean that angels are ministering spirits (Hebrews 1:14)?

The elect angels have a ministry to believers: "Are not all angels ministering spirits sent to serve those who will inherit salvation?" (Hebrews 1:14). Angels are spiritual beings involved in many different tasks, and part of the holy angel's work is to serve, or minister to, believers in different ways.

The Greek word for "ministering" refers to being in service to others. Being servants, angels are said to "serve" believers, which in the original Greek has the idea of someone waiting a table. The author of Hebrews refers to angels as ministers or servants to those who have trusted in Jesus for salvation, and the context of Hebrews 1 specifically contrasts the service of angels with the greater work of Jesus, since He is superior to angels (Hebrews 1:5–14).

As "ministering spirits," angels serve believers in several ways. At times, angels are sent by God to answer prayers. An example of this is when Peter was imprisoned shortly after the execution of James (Acts 12). As Peter was in his cell chained between two guards, "the church was earnestly praying to God for him" (Acts 12:5). "Suddenly an angel of the Lord appeared and a light shone in the cell. He struck Peter on the side and woke him up. 'Quick, get up!' he said, and the chains fell off Peter's wrists" (Acts 12:7). The arrival of an angel to rescue Peter was an obvious answer to the church's prayer. God can use angels to answer our prayers just as He did in this instance, even if the angel does not manifest visibly.

God's ministering spirits are sometimes sent to encourage believers. In Scripture, angels encouraged and attended the Lord Jesus at least twice: after He was tempted in the desert for forty days and forty nights (Matthew 4:11) and as He prayed in the Garden of Gethsemane (Luke 22:43). Paul was encouraged by an angel during a storm at sea (Acts 27:23–24).

Providing protection for believers is another service that angels perform (see Psalm 91:11). An army of angels surrounded Elisha in 2 Kings 6, protecting him from the Arameans. Daniel was protected in the lions' den by an angel who "shut the mouths of the lions" (Daniel 6:22). Many people believe in personal "guardian angels"; it could be that every believer has an angel assigned to him for protection, but there is nothing specifically stated in the Bible about personal guardian angels.

We can praise the Lord for the ministries that angels carry out for believers, since it is the Lord of hosts, our Savior, who sends the angels. Angels do not act on their own accord, nor are they omniscient or omnipresent (Psalm 148:5). The holy angels do God's bidding. It is God alone who deserves the praise and glory for the answered prayers, encouragement, protection, and service that angels perform for believers.

For all their power and glory, the elect angels know their role as servants of the Most High. The angel in Revelation emphatically refused to receive worship. When John the apostle fell down at his feet to worship him, the angel said, "Don't do that! I am a fellow servant with you and with your fellow prophets and with all who keep the words of this scroll. Worship God!" (Revelation 22:9).

14. What does it mean that angels long to look into these things (1 Peter 1:12)?

Peter writes to encourage and admonish believers suffering terrible persecution. He emphasizes his gratitude for Christ's mercy, resurrection, and salvation. In Christ we have an eternal inheritance, a living hope, and inexpressible joy. He reminds believers that their suffering and trials are temporary and serve to strengthen and refine their faith (1 Peter 1:6–7). Following this introduction, Peter makes an interesting statement regarding both prophets and angels:

> Concerning this salvation, the prophets, who spoke of the grace that was to come to you, searched intently and with the greatest care, trying to find out the time and circumstances to which the Spirit of Christ in them was pointing when he predicted the sufferings of the Messiah and the glories that would follow. It was revealed to them that they were not serving themselves but you, when they spoke of the things that have now been told you by those who have preached the gospel to you by the Holy Spirit sent from heaven. Even angels long to look into these things.
>
> 1 Peter 1:10–12

Peter reminds the New Testament believers that they are the recipients of the prophets' scrupulous documentation and attention to Christ's redemption. Even as they wrote of the Messiah's suffering and glorification, the prophets did not fully understand what would happen or when it would happen. They desired to know the object to which Scripture pointed. New Testament believers now understand the gospel and the salvation about which the prophets had spoken.

Peter then says something unexpected about the angels: "Even angels long to look into these things." That is, they are curious about the gospel and how and why it was procured. The angels live in the presence of God, so why would they be interested in human salvation (Matthew 18:10; 22:30)?

Believers in Jesus Christ understand what it is like to be dead in sin and alienated from God (Ephesians 2:1–3). They also understand the overwhelming grace and mercy shown in Christ when He died in their place (Ephesians 2:13). They are adopted into the family of God and have become heirs of God (Romans 8:14–17). Angels, on the other hand, do not know the sweetness of redemption. They have no experiential knowledge of grace and salvation. Angels in heaven have not been separated from God, nor have they personally known reconciliation or the depth of intimacy that follows. It is a foreign concept that piques their curiosity. The Greek word for "to look into" means "to physically stoop down, peer intently, and inspect curiously." Over the course of human history, angels have had a front-row seat in watching God's redemptive work on behalf of humanity (1 Timothy 3:16). The book of Hebrews describes them as "ministering spirits sent out to serve for the sake of those who are to inherit salvation" (Hebrews 1:14 ESV). They are amazed by salvation and lean in attentively, longing to understand its mysteries.

It is important to note that the angels who disobeyed God are not restored or redeemed like humanity is. The Son of God became a man to redeem humanity; He did not become an angel to redeem the heavenly host. Angels cannot fully understand salvation, as it is not for them.

In the book of Exodus, we see further evidence of angelic interest in God's mercy. God commands that the figures of cherubim on the lid of the ark of the covenant were "to have their wings spread upward, overshadowing the cover with them. The cherubim are to face each other, looking toward the cover" (Exodus 25:20; cf. Numbers 7:89; 1 Kings 8:7–8; Hebrews 9:5). The mercy seat represents God's throne; it is where His presence dwelt and the blood of the atonement was offered for sin. The gold cherubim on the ark were placed as if gazing upon God's redemptive purposes. In 1 Peter, angels long to understand the immeasurable glory found in Christ's atonement for sin.

The fact that angels long to look into things pertaining to our salvation is a poignant reminder of what a precious gift salvation is. May we long for salvation and cherish the wonder of redemption!

SECTION 3

Questions About What Angels Are Like

15. What do angels look like?

Angels are spirit beings (Hebrews 1:14), so they do not have any essential physical form. But angels do have the ability to appear in human form. When angels appeared as humans in the Bible, they resembled normal males. In Genesis 18:1–19, God and two angels appeared as men and actually ate a meal with Abraham. Angels appear as men many times throughout the Bible (Joshua 5:13–14; Mark 16:5). They never appear in the likeness of women.

At times, angels appeared not as humans, but as something otherworldly, and their appearance was terrifying to those who encountered them. Often, the first words from these angels were, "Do not be afraid," because extreme fear was such a common reaction. The keepers of Jesus' tomb became as dead men when they saw an angel of the Lord (Matthew 28:4). The shepherds in the fields of Bethlehem were "greatly afraid" when "an angel of the Lord stood before them, and the glory of the Lord shone around them" (Luke 2:9 NKJV).

As for physical characteristics, angels are sometimes described as winged. The images of cherubim on the ark of the covenant had wings that covered the mercy seat (Exodus 25:20). Isaiah saw winged seraphim in his vision of God's throne—each angelic being had six wings, but they also had human features such as faces and feet (Isaiah 6:1–2). Ezekiel saw a vision of a huge cloud filled with lightning and fire. "In the fire was what looked like four living creatures. In appearance their form was human, but each of them had four faces and four wings. Their . . . feet were like those of a calf and gleamed like burnished bronze" (Ezekiel 1:5–7). Each had the face of a human, as well as the faces of a lion, ox, and eagle (v. 10).

Whatever appearance angels take on, there is reason to believe they are incredibly beautiful. Ezekiel tells us that a "guardian cherub" was lifted up in pride over his beauty (Ezekiel 28:16–17). An angel at Jesus' tomb is described as shining brilliantly: "His appearance was like lightning, and his clothes were white as snow" (Matthew 28:3). Beings such as angels, who are continually in the presence of God, would be expected to have extraordinary beauty because God's glory is reflected upon all that is around Him.

16. Are angels male or female?

The question of whether angels are male or female is likely moot. Angels are spirit beings (Hebrews 1:14), and therefore assigning them a gender is pointless. The most we can say is that Scripture *depicts* angels as if they were male.

Every reference to angels in Scripture is in the masculine gender. The Greek word for "angel" in the New Testament, *angelos*, is in the masculine form. In fact, a feminine form of *angelos* does not exist. There are three genders in grammar—masculine (*he, him, his*), feminine (*she, her, hers*), and neuter (*it, its*). Angels are never referred to in any gender other than masculine. In the many appearances of angels in the Bible, never is an angel referred to as "she" or "it." Furthermore, when angels appeared in human form, they were always dressed as males (Genesis 18:2, 16; Ezekiel 9:2). No angel ever appears in Scripture dressed as a female.

The only named angels in the Bible—Michael and Gabriel—are referred to in the masculine. "Michael and his angels" (Revelation 12:7); "Mary was greatly troubled at his [Gabriel's] words" (Luke 1:29). Other references to angels are always in the masculine gender. In Judges 6:21, the angel holds a staff in "his" hand. Zechariah asks an angel a question and reports that "he" answered (Zechariah 1:19). The angels in Revelation are all spoken of as "he" and their possessions as "his" (Revelation 10:1, 5; 14:19; 16:2, 4, 17; 19:17 NKJV; 20:1). The devil, whom we assume is a fallen angel, is also referred to in masculine terms: He is a "father" in John 8:44.

Some people point to Zechariah 5:9 as an example of female angels. That verse says, "Then I looked up—and there before me were two women, with the wind in their wings! They had wings like those of a stork, and they lifted up the basket between heaven and earth." The problem is that the "women" in this prophetic vision are not called angels. They are called in Hebrew *nashiym* ("women"), as is the woman in the basket representing wickedness in verses 7 and 8. By contrast, the angel that Zechariah was speaking to is called a *malak*, a completely different word meaning "angel" or "messenger." The fact that the women have wings in Zechariah's vision might suggest angels to our minds, but we must be careful about going beyond what the text actually says. A vision does not necessarily depict actual beings or objects—consider the huge flying scroll Zechariah sees earlier in the same chapter (Zechariah 5:1–2).

In Matthew 22:30 Jesus says that there will be no marriage in heaven because we "will be like the angels in heaven." This verse states that angels do not marry, but it stops short of commenting on their "gender." Nothing in Jesus' statement can be taken to imply that angels are masculine, feminine, or neuter.

God is spirit (John 4:24) and does not have a "gender" any more than the angels do. At the same time, God almost always refers to Himself in masculine terms. The exceptions are in certain metaphors and in a couple of constructions in which the Holy Spirit is referred to with a neuter intensive pronoun, in grammatical agreement with the Greek neuter noun *pneuma* ("spirit"). In like manner, Scripture refers to angels, which are spirit beings, using masculine terminology.

17. Do angels have wings?

The most common image of an angel is essentially a human being with wings. This is not a biblical image. The Bible often presents angels as appearing as human beings. But this does not indicate that angels in their essence look like us. The Bible describes two types of angels as having wings: the four-winged cherubim (Exodus 25:20; Ezekiel 10) and the six-winged seraphim (Isaiah 6). Cherubim and seraphim are possibly the two highest orders of angels.

Angels are spirit beings (Hebrews 1:14). The descriptions of the cherubim in Ezekiel chapter 10 and the seraphim in Isaiah chapter 6 are otherworldly. Ezekiel, especially, seems to have struggled to accurately describe the vision he saw. The "living creatures" he wrote of had wings, although, as spirit beings, it is unclear why they would need them. Surely spirit beings do not require wings to fly, since they are not bound by the laws of the physical universe.

So, do angels have wings? Yes, some angels do have wings. However, we should not limit what angels can or cannot do based on our limited understanding of the wings some angels possess as described in the Bible.

18. Do angels sing?

It may seem strange to ask if angels sing; conventional wisdom says, "Of course they do." It's common to see pictures of angels holding songbooks or harps or otherwise engaged in music-making. And people often point to the Christmas story, under the impression that the angels sang to the shepherds when Jesus was born. The Christmas carol "Hark! The Herald Angels Sing" certainly contributes to the idea of an angelic choir making melody in the heavens. But the fact remains that the biblical Christmas story does not mention singing. In fact, there is very little scriptural evidence that the angels sing.

One passage that touches on this question is Job 38:7, which says that, at the creation of the world, "the morning stars sang together and all the angels shouted for joy." In the parallelism of the Hebrew poetry, "morning stars" are equated with "angels," and the singing is paralleled by the joyful shouts. It seems fairly straightforward: The angels sing. However, the Hebrew word translated "sang" doesn't always denote music. It can also be translated as "joyfully shouted," "resoundingly cried," or "rejoiced." Also, the word translated "angels" in the NIV literally means "sons of God."

Revelation 5 is another passage that may indicate that the angels sing. Verse 9 speaks of beings that "sang a new song" in heaven. These beings that sing are the twenty-four elders and the four living creatures—the four living creatures are possibly angelic beings, but they are not specifically called such. Then "the voice of many angels" is heard (Revelation 5:12). But now the action is described as "saying" the words, not specifically "singing" them. The words of the angelic host in verse 12 are similar to the words of the song in verse 9, but what the angels say is not explicitly called a song. So, there is no conclusive proof in Revelation 5 that angels sing.

What about the Christmas story? Luke 2:13–14 says, "Suddenly a great company of the heavenly host appeared with the angel, praising God and saying, 'Glory to God. . . .'" As in Revelation 5, the words of the angels are "said," not specifically "sung." Since singing is a type of speaking, the passage does not rule out the idea that the angels sang—but neither does the passage put the question to rest.

In short, the Bible does not give a definitive answer as to whether the angels sing. God has created humanity with an innate connection to music and singing, especially in regard to worship (Ephesians 5:19). We often use singing when we praise the Lord. The fact that the angelic praise in Revelation 5 and Luke 2 is expressed in poetic form argues for the idea that the angels are singing. And it would seem logical that God created the angels with the same propensity for singing as humans have. But we cannot be dogmatic. Whether the angels were singing or speaking in the Bible, they were worshiping and praising God. May we follow their example!

19. Can angels reproduce?

Angels have been the subject of story, song, and folklore since time began. And, while angels are a reality—the Bible speaks of them often—much of what we imagine about them is total fiction. Angels have never been human, and humans do not become angels when they die. Angels are not fat babies with wings or beautiful women with an ethereal glow. Angels are spirit beings, created by God to serve Him and humanity (Hebrews 1:14). In the Bible's descriptions of their visits to earth, angels always appear as men (Daniel 9:21; Luke 1:26; Matthew 28:1–7). The Bible never describes a female angel. Some questions arise: Is there a set number of angels? Is it possible for angels to reproduce?

The Bible never directly says that angels do or do not reproduce, but Jesus touched on a related subject. When asked about human marriage in eternity, Jesus replied, "At the resurrection people will neither marry nor be given in marriage; they will be like the angels in heaven" (Matthew 22:30). The fact that there is no marriage among angels has led some to believe that angels are "sexless" or genderless. Of course, if angels are genderless, then a safe assumption is that they do not reproduce—but that conclusion cannot be *proved* from the text. The fact that there is no marriage among angels does not *necessarily* mean there is no gender and no procreation. Angels do not marry, but we can't make the leap from "no marriage" to "no gender" or "no reproduction," however logical such a leap would seem.

One passage that might refer to the angels' ability to reproduce is found in Genesis 6:1–4. Scholars have debated for centuries whether the "sons of God" mentioned here were angels. If they were, they might be identified with the fallen angels in Jude 1:6 who had left their primary purpose and defiled themselves, an act for which they were harshly judged. It could be that rebellious angelic spirits took on human form to the extent that they could engage in sexual union with human women and produce offspring who were only half-human. Some scholars speculate that this subhuman (or superhuman) race was the mighty "men of renown" referred to as Nephilim in Genesis 6:4. Because of the contamination of the human race, God sent the flood to annihilate them all (Genesis 6:5–7). However, since the Bible gives little detail about it, we can only speculate and should not base any doctrine on those speculations. Even if the Nephilim were the product of unnatural angelic-human unions, it would not answer the question of whether angels reproduce with other angels to create new angels.

Angels who dwell in the presence of God live to serve and worship Him. The Bible never hints at the idea that angels reproduce or that they have any need to. As far as we know, angels do not die, so angel reproduction is not necessary to continue the race of angelic beings. God created angels, He sustains them, and, if He desires more angels, He can create them.

20. Do angels have souls?

We may never have all the answers about angels, but their appearances throughout Scripture give many insights into who they are and what they do. Whether angels have souls is not addressed in the Bible, but we can hypothesize.

God created angels, just as He created everything else (Colossians 1:16). He commands, and they obey (Psalm 91:11; 103:20–21). They fight for God and protect His people (2 Kings 6:16–17; Psalm 91:11–12; Daniel 6:22; Matthew 26:53). They also act as messengers, bringing the word of God to people through dreams, visions, or simply by appearing before them (Matthew 1:20; 2:13; Luke 1:11–20; Acts 1:10–11; 8:26). We know that angels are spiritual beings, as Scripture describes them as "ministering spirits sent to serve those who will inherit salvation" (Hebrews 1:14). The holy angels worship God (Job 38:7; Psalm 148:2; Luke 2:13–14; Revelation 5:11–12), but they do not receive worship for themselves (Revelation 19:10). While all these characteristics are remarkable, they do not answer questions about angels' souls.

The Bible leaves the exact nature of the soul a mystery; however, we can surmise that the soul is a central part of our personhood. People themselves are referred to as "souls" (Acts 2:41 NKJV). A human's soul is immaterial and immortal; it persists after the human body dies (Daniel 12:2; 2 Corinthians 5:8–9). Angels are personal, spiritual beings (Hebrews 1:14), and they are immortal (Luke 20:36). However, Scripture never refers to angels as "souls," and it seems the immaterial nature of angels is not the same thing as the immaterial human soul. Human beings are unique among creation because they are made in the image of God (Genesis 1:27). Angels are a separate order of being, different from humans. People will not turn into angels at death, and angels will never become human. This clear distinction and the centrality of the soul in human life would seem to indicate that angels do not have souls.

There are other biblical hints that angels are without souls. Human souls need atonement (Leviticus 17:11 NKJV), God protects and purifies souls (Titus 3:5; Hebrews 10:21–22), and a soul can be either lost or saved (Ezekiel 18:4; James 1:21). None of these qualities of the soul apply to angels. Angels do not need to be purified, atoned for, or saved. Hebrews 1–2 describes how Jesus is superior to angels and teaches that His salvation is for humans, not angels: "The Son did not come to help angels; he came to help the descendants of Abraham" (Hebrews 2:16 NLT). The angels worship Jesus (Hebrews 1:6). God "makes his angels spirits, and his servants flames of fire" (Hebrews 1:7). Holy angels serve those who are saved (Hebrews 1:14), but they themselves do not need salvation. This may be a further indication that angels do not have souls.

A point of clarification is in order. It is true that there are fallen angels who do not serve God and are, in fact, His enemies. We might think that these fallen angels need "salvation"; however, there is no indication in the Bible that they would ever seek to repent or that God has provided a way of salvation for them. They will be judged (2 Peter 2:4), and they will be cast with Satan into the lake of fire for all eternity (Matthew 25:41). Humans, on the other hand, do have the opportunity to avoid judgment through the blood of Jesus Christ (Ephesians 2:1–10; Romans 8:1; 10:9–13; John 3:16–18; 1 John 2:2). All who turn to God and put their faith in Jesus will be saved. Praise God that, in His grace, He has made a way for us to be saved and to dwell with Him forever (Revelation 21:1–4; John 14:3; Philippians 1:21–23).

21. Do angels have free will?

Although the Bible mentions angels over 250 times, the references are usually incidental to some other topic. Learning what the Bible has to say about angels can certainly aid in an understanding of

God and His ways, but what is learned about the angels themselves must usually be drawn from implicit, rather than explicit, descriptions.

Angels are spiritual beings who have personalities that include emotions (Luke 2:13–14), intelligence (2 Corinthians 11:3, 14), and wills (2 Timothy 2:26). Satan was an angel who was cast out of heaven along with many other angels who decided to follow him and *chose* to sin (2 Peter 2:4). Satan's will is mentioned directly in 2 Timothy 2:26. The Bible speaks of demons who, by their own *choice*, "did not keep their positions of authority but abandoned their proper dwelling" (Jude 1:6). Demons demonstrate their free will in several passages of Scripture. Legion *chose* a herd of pigs as their destination (Luke 8:32). In Micaiah's vision of God's throne room, God allows a spirit to *choose* how to bring ruin upon King Ahab (1 Kings 22:19–22).

Before some of the angels exercised their free will to rebel against God, they could have been in a sort of probation period, similar to Adam and Eve's time in the garden. Those angels who did not choose to sin and follow Satan have become the "elect" angels (1 Timothy 5:21), confirmed in holiness. These angels are also referred to as "holy angels" (Mark 8:38) and "holy ones" (Psalm 89:5). Those angels who did choose to sin in siding with Satan have become the "impure" spirits (Mark 1:23), or demons.

Even if the elect angels are confirmed in their holiness, it doesn't mean they have lost their free will. Certainly, every living creature has choices to make at any given moment. It's possible that the holy angels still have the ability to sin, but that does not mean that they will sin. Being holy angels, they always do God's bidding. Being volitional creatures, the elect angels have a desire to praise and serve God, and they choose to do so. Their will always matches God's will.

Humans have free will, but they struggle with sin because the human nature has been corrupted by sin. This is why all humans sin (Romans 5:12) and find it much more difficult to "be good" than to "be bad." The holy angels are without a sinful nature. They are not inclined toward sin but rather toward righteousness, doing everything that pleases God.

In conclusion, the holy angels have a free will, but the Bible makes it clear that they do not sin in their service to God. The apostle John, in describing the eternal state, wrote there will be no mourning, crying, or pain in that place and time (Revelation 21:4), and anyone who does evil will never be permitted to enter the city of God (Revelation 21:27). The angels who are present in that holy city are therefore sinless.

22. In what ways are angels and humans different?

Angels have captured the human imagination since the beginning of time. Perhaps the most intriguing quality of angels is that they sometimes abandon their unseen existence in the spirit realm to take on human resemblance and interact with us. For many reasons, angels fascinate humans. Angels are different from us; they are unique creations of God that, at present, can only be effectively perceived through the lens of Scripture.

The words for "angel" in Hebrew and Greek signify a "messenger," which designates the office or official function of such a being. Angels were created to be God's messengers, sent out to serve His purposes. In some ways, angels are like humans. They are superior beings created by God with intelligence, morality, and spirituality. They worship God and carry out His will (Psalm 103:20). Like humans, angels possess limited knowledge (Matthew 24:36), although the Bible indicates that angels have greater knowledge and higher rank than humans (Hebrews 2:7–9; Mark 13:32). One purpose of angels is to serve God's people (Hebrews 1:14). God commissions angels to protect His people (Psalm 91:11–12), deliver them from danger (2 Kings 19:35), transmit divine messages (Hebrews 2:2), give guidance (Exodus 23:20), and encourage believers (1 Kings 19:5–7).

The Bible reveals a host of ways angels are different from humans. Angels are spirit beings (Hebrews 1:14), meaning they do not have a physical body. Humans are set apart from all other created beings because they have both a material body and an immaterial soul or spirit. Since angels are immaterial and incorporeal, they do not experience physical suffering and harm like human beings do, nor do they experience physical death (Luke 20:36).

God is also a Spirit being, but His nature is infinite, while angels are finite spirit beings. The spiritual nature of angels does not prevent them from making their presence known to humans; usually, when they appear to people, angels portray themselves in the form of human men (Daniel 8:16; 9:21). They have appeared to people in visions and dreams (Matthew 1:20; Isaiah 6:1–8) and in a conscious, awakened state (Genesis 19:1–8; Mark 16:5; Luke 2:13).

The Bible often ascribes to angels superhuman characteristics quite different from what ordinary people possess. In various places, certain types of angels are said to have "eyes like flaming torches," legs "like fiery pillars," and "six wings" (Daniel 10:5–7; Revelation 10:1–3; Isaiah 6:2). Angels are "far greater in power and strength" than humans (2 Peter 2:11 NLT; see also 2 Thessalonians 1:7). Angels wage spiritual warfare (Ephesians 6:12).

The author of Hebrews stresses angels' swift and subtle nature as they perform God's will: "He sends his angels like the winds, his servants like flames of fire" (Hebrews 1:7 NLT). In Peter's dramatic escape from prison, a brightly lit angel appeared out of nowhere, released chains, slipped undetected by the guards, passed through heavy iron gates, and set the apostle free before he knew what had hit him. Just as suddenly, the angel disappeared (Acts 12:6–10).

Unlike humans, who are born with a sin nature (Romans 5:12), all angels were created originally as holy creatures (Jude 1:6; see also Ezekiel 28:15). Some were "the elect angels" who remained faithful to God (1 Timothy. 5:21), while others exercised their free will to rebel against God and sinned (2 Peter 2:4). Christian theology proposes that angels underwent a sort of probationary test in which all had the opportunity to remain in their original state of holiness. The elect—those who successfully passed the test and did not rebel—were confirmed in holiness forever. Those who failed became "impure" spirits, or demons (Mark 1:23; cf. Luke 8:2; 11:24), and are now confirmed in their evil, rebellious state.

Angels differ from humans in that they are not the objects of God's salvation (1 Peter 1:10–12). Although they cannot experience God's saving grace themselves, angels are intensely interested in its application to humans (Luke 15:10; 1 Corinthians 4:9; Ephesians 3:10). Only humans are created in God's image (Genesis 1:26–27) to be conformed to the likeness of His Son, Jesus Christ (Romans 8:29). The rebellious angels were not given an opportunity for their sins to be forgiven. Instead, they are awaiting "the eternal fire prepared for the devil and his angels" (Matthew 25:41). Humans, however, can be forgiven of their sins and redeemed by God's grace through faith in the Lord Jesus Christ (Ephesians 2:8–9; Romans 10:9–10). Humans were made "a little lower than the angels" (Hebrews 2:7, 9). Yet, once saved, resurrected, and glorified, believers will judge the angels (1 Corinthians 6:3).

Angels and humans are decidedly different, though they share some similarities. Angels are not our dearly departed loved ones. They are not people who have died, nor are they glorified humans (Hebrews 12:22–23). Jesus taught that angels do not marry as humans do (Matthew 22:30). Angels (and not humans) were present when the earth was created, and they shouted joyfully to God (Job 38:4–7). Although angels are special and unique creations of their own, only humans are recipients of God's redeeming love, as demonstrated through Jesus Christ (John 3:16).

23. Can angels die?

We have many more questions about angels and demons than we have answers. Many times we have to make guesses and assumptions based on a few biblical facts. Frank Peretti's popular novel *This Present Darkness* had angelic beings crossing swords and demons disappearing in puffs of red smoke when they were slashed in two. It made for a fun read, but there was more imagination than biblical precision in Peretti's pages.

Angels are essentially spiritual beings without bodies. Hebrews 1:14 calls them ministering spirits. When they appear to people, they normally are seen with bodies. Sometimes they appear as ordinary men (Hebrews 13:2) or incredibly glorious men (Daniel 10:5–6) and sometimes as fantastic creatures (Isaiah 6:2; Ezekiel 1:4–14). However, since angels do not have bodies, these forms are only manifestations in material/visible form. They do not represent what the angel actually "looks like" because a spirit is essentially invisible, at least to the physical eye. Angels sometimes appear with wings in Scripture and are often depicted with wings in art, but physical wings are used to move physical bodies through physical air, and, again, angels are spirit beings.

Since angels do not have physical bodies, they cannot be hurt in the sense of suffering physical harm in the same way a human being with a body could be hurt. Angels cannot die in that sense, either. Physical death is something that humans experience when their bodies cease working and their spirits depart from their bodies. Since angels do not have physical bodies, they cannot experience physical death.

It is possible that angels do encounter some perils in the spiritual world, perils that are beyond our normal experience or comprehension. An angel was sent with an answer to Daniel's prayer but was detained by a being called "the prince of the Persian kingdom" (a fallen angel/demon) and prevented from coming to Daniel for twenty-one days (Daniel 10:12–13). How was the angel detained? We are not told. Even though they are spirits, angels are not omnipresent, so they do have some kind of localized existence that apparently can be contained. When angels "fight" with demons, do they get injured by each other? Perhaps, but we are simply not told what this type of fighting entails. When we are in battle with spiritual forces, we do not use physical weapons but the armor of God detailed in Ephesians 6:10–18.

If demons are fallen angels, then we know that angels can suffer. When Jesus cast demons out, they sometimes feared that Jesus was going to torture or torment them (see Matthew 8:29; Luke 8:28). Legion begged Jesus not to send them into the Abyss, a holding place for fallen angels/demons (Luke 8:31). If they feared going there, they must be able to suffer in some way. At the final judgment, all the fallen angels will be cast into the lake of fire (Matthew 25:41). How can a spiritual being be tormented by flames of fire? We don't know. As spiritual beings who were meant to enjoy fellowship with God, isolation from God will result in the worst kind of torture.

As mentioned at the beginning of this response, we have many more questions than answers. As beings bound by time and space, we have difficulty imagining the experience of spiritual beings.

24. If angels and demons can't die, what is the point of their engaging in battle?

Popular fiction, such as the novel *This Present Darkness* by Frank Peretti, often features lurid descriptions of spiritual battles in which demons are dispatched by sword-wielding angels with a slash, a flash, and a puff of smoke. The implication is that the demons "die" somehow when sliced in half by angelic blades. It should go without saying that our theology should be based on what the Bible says, not contemporary novels. The Bible teaches the reality of spiritual battle (Jude 1:9). But the Bible also says that, after the final judgment, demons will be consigned forever to the lake of fire (Matthew 25:41). Since demons (and angels) do not "die" or suffer physical wounds, what is the point of doing spiritual battle?

First, we need to remember that not all battles are "to the death." The angels' goal in battling demons is not to kill them but to thwart their plans and further God's plans. In the Bible, we see that angels do battle with demons in order to deliver divine messages to people (Daniel 10:12–14) and remove Satan's hordes from heavenly places (Revelation 12:7–8). Demons can be withstood (James 4:7), tortured by God (Luke 8:28), lose what they possess (Mark 9:25–26), be sent to another place (Matthew 8:32), and be removed to the Abyss (Luke 8:31).

Second, there will be a time when Satan and his demons will experience what the Bible calls "the second death," which is the lake of fire (Revelation 21:8). We look forward to that day because the demons' main objective in battle is to counter God's will in the lives of people everywhere—believers and nonbelievers alike (1 Peter 5:8). We have many examples in the Bible of God sending His angels to warn, guide, and protect His children. Some great examples are in the Christmas story. God used angels to inform Zechariah that he would have a son named John (Luke 1:8–20), to tell Mary that she would bear the Messiah (Luke 1:26–38), to declare Christ's birth to shepherds (Luke 2:8–12), and to warn Joseph to protect his family from King Herod's wrath (Matthew 2:13).

God has not seen fit to imprison all demons just yet, but He promises that in the end they, along with Satan, will be thrown into the lake of fire. There is no escape from this fate, and all demonic spirits will be tormented in eternal isolation from God (Revelation 20:10).

The reality of spiritual warfare affects every believer. It is important to recognize this warfare is taking place and be prepared for it. God has given us all that is necessary to stand firm against the devil's schemes and has commanded us to put on the full spiritual armor (Ephesians 6:10–18).

SECTION 4

Questions About Types of Angels

25. What are the different types of angels?

Angels fall into two categories: the "unfallen" angels and the fallen angels. Unfallen angels are those who have remained sinless throughout their existence and accordingly are called "holy angels." Generally, when angels are mentioned in Scripture, it is the class of holy angels in view. By contrast, the fallen angels are those who sinned and rebelled against God.

Holy angels seem to be divided into special classes, and certain ones are named. Michael the archangel is likely the head of all the holy angels, and his name means "who is like unto God?" (Daniel 10:21; 12:1; 1 Thessalonians 4:16; Jude 1:9; Revelation 12:7–10). Gabriel is one of the principal messengers of God, his name meaning "hero of God." Gabriel was entrusted with important messages such as those delivered to Daniel (Daniel 8:16; 9:21), Zechariah (Luke 1:18–19), and Mary (Luke 1:26–38).

Most holy angels are not named in the Bible but are described only as "elect angels" (1 Timothy 5:21). The expression *principalities and powers* seems to be used of all angels, whether fallen or holy (Luke 21:26; Romans 8:38; Ephesians 1:21; 3:10; Colossians 1:16; 2:10, 15; 1 Peter 3:22). Some angels are designated as "cherubim" (Genesis 3:24; Exodus 25:18, 20) and others as "seraphim" (Isaiah 6:2–7). The cherubim in Genesis 3:24 are described as having "a flaming sword"; the seraphim in Isaiah 6 have three pairs of wings. Most of the references to holy angels in Scripture refer to their ministries, which are broad. Holy angels are seen delivering messages and protecting God's people. They were present at creation and involved in the giving of the law. Angels announced the birth of Christ, ministered to Jesus during His sojourn on earth, and were present at His resurrection and ascension. They will be seen again at the rapture of the church and the second coming of Christ.

The fallen angels are confirmed in their wickedness, much like the holy angels are confirmed in holiness. Led by Satan, who was originally a cherub, the fallen angels defected from God's service, rebelled against Him, and became corrupt in their nature and work. Fallen angels exist in two states: free and bound. Of the fallen angels, Satan alone is given particular mention in the Bible. When Satan fell (John 8:44; Luke 10:18), he drew after him one third of the angels (see Revelation 12:4). Of those, some are chained, awaiting judgment (1 Corinthians 6:3; 2 Peter 2:4; Jude 1:6); the remainder are free for now and aid the devil in his destructive work. The demons, or unclean spirits, are referenced often in the New Testament (Mark 5:9, 15; Luke 8:30; 1 Timothy 4:1). They will share Satan's doom (Matthew 25:41; Revelation 20:10).

26. How many angels are there?

Only three angels are identified by name in the Bible: Gabriel (Daniel 8:16), Michael the archangel (Daniel 10:13), and Lucifer the fallen angel (Isaiah 14:12 NKJV). Yet angelic beings are mentioned at least 273 times in thirty-four books of the Bible. While we don't know exactly how many angels there are, we do know from Scripture that an exceedingly large number of angels exist.

The book of Hebrews describes a multitude of angels in heaven too great to count: "You have come to Mount Zion, to the city of the living God, the heavenly Jerusalem, and to countless thousands of angels in a joyful gathering" (Hebrews 12:22 NLT). Other Bible translations use terms like "innumerable" (ESV), "myriads" (CSB), and "thousands upon thousands" (NIV) to quantify this enormous throng of angels. The impressive picture expands in the book of Revelation: "Then I looked and heard the voice of many angels, numbering thousands upon thousands, and ten thousand times ten thousand. They encircled the throne and the living creatures and the elders" (Revelation 5:11). Other Bible versions use "myriads of myriads" (ESV) and even "millions" (NLT) here to express how many angels there are in heaven.

While the Bible leaves the precise number of angels unspecified, some believe there could be as many angels in existence as the total number of humans in all of history. This theory is based on Matthew 18:10: "Beware that you don't look down on any of these little ones. For I tell you that in heaven their angels are always in the presence of my heavenly Father" (NLT). The passage seems to suggest that individual people, or at least children, have guardian angels to protect them. It's possible, though, that Jesus was speaking here only in general terms regarding the function of angels as protectors of children. In any case, Scripture is clear that angels do guard and protect human beings (Psalm 34:7; 91:11–12; Matthew 18:10; Acts 12:9–15).

The Bible describes different classifications of angels. Some angels—the cherubim and seraphim—are described as winged creatures. Cherubim primarily attend the throne of God as guards, while it seems the seraphim attend His throne by offering worship and praise (Ezekiel 1:4–28; 10:1–22; Isaiah 6:2–6). The Bible speaks of angels of light (2 Corinthians 11:14) and fallen angels (2 Peter 2:4; Jude 1:6).

Angels perform different tasks in the Bible. All angels are servants of God in some way (Psalm 103:20; Hebrews 1:7; Psalm 104:4). Some angels deliver God's messages (Daniel 4:13). "Watcher" angels (NKJV) are mentioned in the book of Daniel (Daniel 4:13, 17, 23). Angels are often described as military "hosts" (NKJV) of the celestial armies (Jeremiah 5:14; 38:17; 44:7; Hosea 12:5). Other times angels are called "sons of the mighty" (Psalm 89:6 NKJV) or "sons of God" (Job 2:1 NKJV).

A few passages of Scripture describe angels as stars (Revelation 9:1; 12:4; Job 38:7–8; Daniel 8:10; Judges 5:20). The idea of stars may give us our best clue as to how many angels there are. If angels are like the stars in heaven, there are too many to count. Moses says in Deuteronomy 33:2 that the Lord came to speak to him from Sinai with "myriads of holy ones," or angels. How many are myriads? The primary definition of *myriad* as an adjective is "innumerable," or "countless." Psalm 68:17 says the angels of God number "tens of thousands, thousands and thousands" (CSB). Clearly, the writer has trouble even coming close to estimating the number of angels in existence.

27. What is the hierarchy of angels?

Some branches of Christian theology have proposed a nine-level hierarchy of angels as follows:

Highest/First Order:

- Seraphim
- Cherubim
- Thrones

Middle/Second Order:

- Dominions
- Virtues
- Powers

Lowest/Third Order:

- Principalities
- Archangels
- Angels[1]

The difficulty is that the Bible identifies no such hierarchy of angels. In the Bible we see that there *could* be different kinds of angels, and, if there are different kinds, there *might* be some sort of hierarchy. If a hierarchy exists, the Bible does not tell us about it explicitly. If it were important for us to know about it, the Bible would have told us. The term *angel* simply means "messenger" and emphasizes the work that angels do.

Seraphim (singular *seraph*) is simply a word that means "fiery" or "bright." Seraphim are mentioned as angelic beings only in Isaiah 6:1–4:

> I saw the Lord, high and exalted, seated on a throne; and the train of his robe filled the temple. Above him were seraphim, each with six wings: With two wings they covered their faces, with two they covered their feet, and with two they were flying. And they were calling to one another:
>
> "Holy, holy, holy is the LORD Almighty;
> the whole earth is full of his glory."
>
> At the sound of their voices the doorposts and thresholds shook and the temple was filled with smoke.

Since the word *seraphim* is simply a description, it may be that the seraphim are simply "fiery beings" that may or may not be a distinct "kind" of angel.

Cherubim (singular *cherub*) are mentioned numerous times in Scripture. After Adam and Eve were driven out of the Garden of Eden, cherubim were placed there to guard the entrance (Genesis 3:24). The majority of the instances where cherubim are mentioned are in connection with the ark of the covenant, as the likeness of two cherubim adorned the cover of the ark (Exodus 25:18–20; 37:7–9; 1 Samuel 4:4). David sings a song of praise to God in which he says that God "mounted the cherubim and flew; he soared on the wings of the wind" (2 Samuel 22:11). When Ezekiel sees the glory of God leaving the temple, he also sees cherubim carrying the throne of God (Ezekiel 10). In Ezekiel 1:10, the cherubim are described as having four faces, one of a human being, a lion, an ox, and an eagle. However, since angels are essentially spirit beings, it may be that they simply appeared to Ezekiel in this form for that particular revelatory vision.

There is only one archangel named in Scripture: Michael. He is mentioned in Jude 1:9. The voice of the archangel is heard in 1 Thessalonians 4:16, with no mention of his name. Revelation 12:7 describes war between Michael and his angels and the devil and his angels. In Daniel 10:13, 21 and 12:1, Michael is described as an angelic prince. Michael's being the leader of the angels would fit with both the title *archangel* and the role he plays. *Archangel* may be a role rather than a distinct kind of angel.

Another individual angel, Gabriel, is also named in Scripture. Gabriel delivered messages regarding the births of John the Baptist (Luke 1:19) and Jesus (Luke 1:26). In speaking to John's father, Gabriel describes himself as one who stands in the presence of God. There is no mention of what "kind" of angel Gabriel may be. He also delivered messages to Daniel in answer to his prayer (Daniel 8:16; 9:21). Daniel describes him as a man, which means that Gabriel appeared in human form. Again, as angels are essentially spirit beings, they do not have physical bodies, but it seems they may appear in various forms.

Michael and Gabriel are the only angels mentioned by name, but we know there are untold myriads of angels who serve God. It should be noted that, although angels have greater power and glory than human beings, it is human beings who are created in God's image, and it is human beings, not angels, who will reign with Christ (Hebrews 2:5). It is human beings, not angels, who have been redeemed by the blood of Christ (Hebrews 2:16). Angels are servants of God who minister to believers (Hebrews 1:14). From one perspective, angels are certainly greater than people, yet from another perspective, human beings occupy the primary place in God's created order. Angels do not understand redemption in the way that God's children understand it (1 Peter 1:12).

The term *guardian angel* is never mentioned in Scripture, although this concept is commonly assumed. Perhaps it is based on Matthew 18:10: "See that you do not despise one of these little ones. For I tell you that their angels in heaven always see the face of my Father in heaven."

Finally, there are fallen angels. Jude 1:6 mentions some of them: "And the angels who did not keep their positions of authority but abandoned their proper dwelling—these he has kept in darkness, bound with everlasting chains for judgment on the great Day." Others wage war in Revelation 12:7–9: "Then war broke out in heaven. Michael and his angels fought against the dragon, and the dragon and his angels fought back. But he was not strong enough, and they lost their place in heaven. The great dragon was hurled down—that ancient serpent called the devil, or Satan, who leads the whole world astray. He was hurled to the earth, and his angels with him."

Speculation abounds, but there is no elaborate hierarchy of angels revealed in Scripture. Angels simply serve in the background and bring glory to God.

28. What are archangels?

The word *archangel* occurs in only two verses of the Bible. First Thessalonians 4:16 says, "For the Lord himself will come down from heaven, with a loud command, with the voice of the archangel and with the trumpet call of God, and the dead in Christ will rise first." The other passage is Jude 1:9: "But even the archangel Michael, when he was disputing with the devil about the body of Moses, did not himself dare to condemn him for slander but said, 'The Lord rebuke you!'" Michael is the only named archangel in Scripture.

The word *archangel* comes from a Greek word, *archangelos,* meaning "chief angel." It's a compound word formed from *archon* ("chief" or "ruler") and *aggelos* ("angel" or "messenger"). The Bible suggests in several places that angels have a hierarchy of leadership, and an archangel seems to be the leader of other angels.

Like all angels, archangels are personal beings created by God. They possess intelligence, power, and glory. They are spiritual in nature, rather than corporeal. Archangels serve God and carry out His purposes.

Jude 1:9 uses the definite article *the* when referring to the archangel Michael, which could indicate that Michael is the only archangel. However, Daniel 10:13 describes Michael as "one of the chief princes." This possibly indicates that there is more than one archangel, because it places Michael on the same level as the other "chief princes." So, while it is possible that there are multiple archangels, it is best not to presume upon the Word of God by declaring other angels as archangels. Even if there are multiple archangels, it seems that Michael is the chief among them.

In Daniel 10:21 an angel describes Michael the archangel as "your prince." Since the angel is speaking to Daniel, and since Daniel is a Jew, we take the angel's statement to mean that Michael is charged with overseeing the Jewish people. Daniel 12:1 confirms this interpretation, calling Michael "the great prince who protects your [Daniel's] people." Perhaps other archangels are given the task of protecting other nations, but Scripture does not identify them. Fallen angels seem to have "territories" as well, as Daniel 10:20 mentions a spiritual "prince of Greece" and a spiritual "prince of Persia" who oppose the holy angel who brought the message to Daniel.

One of the duties of an archangel, as seen in Daniel 10, is to engage in spiritual warfare. In 1 Thessalonians 4, the archangel is involved in the return of Christ for His church. We also see Michael the archangel contending with Satan in Jude 1:9. Even possessing the power and glory of an archangel, Michael called on the Lord to rebuke Satan. This shows how powerful Satan is, as well as how dependent Michael is on God's power. If the archangel looks to the Lord for his help, should we do any less?

29. What are cherubim?

Cherubim/cherubs are angelic beings involved in the worship and praise of God. The cherubim are first mentioned in the Bible in Genesis 3:24, "After he drove the man out, he placed on the east side of the Garden of Eden cherubim and a flaming sword flashing back and forth to guard the way to the tree of life." Prior to his rebellion, Satan was a cherub (Ezekiel 28:12–15). The tabernacle and temple along with their articles contained many representations of cherubim (Exodus 25:17–22; 26:1, 31; 36:8; 1 Kings 6:23–35; 7:29–36; 8:6–7; 1 Chronicles 28:18; 2 Chronicles 3:7–14; 2 Chronicles 3:10–13; 5:7–8; Hebrews 9:5).

Chapters 1 and 10 of the book of Ezekiel describe the "four living creatures" (Ezekiel 1:5) as the same beings as the cherubim (Ezekiel 10). Each had four faces—that of a man, a lion, an ox, and an eagle (Ezekiel 1:10; see also 10:14–15)—and each had four wings. In their appearance, the cherubim "had the likeness of a man" (Ezekiel 1:5 NKJV). These cherubim used two of their wings for flying and the other two for covering their bodies (Ezekiel 1:6, 11, 23). Under their wings the cherubim appeared to have the form, or likeness, of a man's hand (Ezekiel 1:8; 10:7–8, 21).

The imagery of Revelation 4:6–9 also seems to be describing cherubim. The cherubim serve the purpose of magnifying the holiness and power of God. This is one of their main responsibilities throughout the Bible. In addition to praising God, they also serve as a visible reminder of the majesty and glory of God and His abiding presence with His people.

30. What are seraphim?

The seraphim ("fiery, burning ones") are angelic beings associated with the prophet Isaiah's vision of God in the temple (Isaiah 6:1–7). Isaiah describes the scene:

> Above [the Lord] were seraphim, each with six wings: With two wings they covered their faces, with two they covered their feet, and with two they were flying. And they were calling to one another:
>
> "Holy, holy, holy is the LORD Almighty;
> the whole earth is full of his glory."
>
> At the sound of their voices the doorposts and thresholds shook and the temple was filled with smoke.
>
> Isaiah 6:2–4

It would seem from this passage that seraphs are angels who worship God continually.

Isaiah chapter 6 is the only place in the Bible that specifically mentions the seraphim. Each seraph had six wings. Nineteenth-century

Scottish pastor Alexander MacLaren, in his *Expositions of Holy Scripture*, saw the three pairs of wings as carrying special significance:

- Wings of reverence (the wings covering the faces of the seraphim)
- Wings of humility (the wings covering the feet of the seraphim)
- Wings of service (the wings with which they flew)[2]

The seraphim flew about the throne where God was seated, shouting His praises as they called special attention to God's holiness, glory, and majesty. The voices of these beings were so powerful that the temple was shaken to its very foundation. These seraphim apparently also served as agents of purification for Isaiah as he began his prophetic ministry. One of them flew to the altar, took a hot coal, and placed it against Isaiah's lips with the words, "See, this has touched your lips; your guilt is taken away and your sin atoned for" (Isaiah 6:7).

Along with the other types of holy angels, the seraphim are perfectly obedient to God.

31. Who are the four living creatures in Revelation?

The four living creatures are found in Revelation 4:6–9; 5:6–14; 6:1–8; 14:3; 15:7; and 19:4. The texts that describe these creatures indicate that they are actual beings. The four living creatures (literally, "beings") are a special, exalted order of angelic being, probably cherubim. They stand close to the throne of God. Ezekiel 1:12–20 depicts what are likely the same creatures moving or standing still as they follow the promptings of the Spirit of God.

Revelation 5:6–14 describes the duties or purposes of the four living creatures. They fall down and worship the Lamb, Jesus Christ, offering the same reverence to Him that they did to the Father (Revelation 4:6–9), proof positive of the deity of Jesus Christ. Along with the twenty-four elders, they have harps and "golden bowls full of incense, which are the prayers of God's people" (Revelation 5:8). Harps are frequently associated with both worship and prophecy in the Old Testament (2 Kings 3:15; 1 Chronicles 25:1). The burning incense is identified as representing the prayers of the saints ascending toward God. So, the four living creatures and twenty-four elders hold in their hands all that prophets ever prophesied and believers ever prayed—and it's all about to come to pass.

The four living creatures also declare the holiness of God and lead in worship and adoration of God. In addition, they seem to be involved in some way with God's justice, for when the Lamb opens the first four seals, releasing the four horsemen, the powerful voices of the living creatures issue a thunderous command to "come" (Revelation 6:1–8). The horsemen respond to the summons and go forth to accomplish their tasks in the world. The power of the four living creatures is seen again in Revelation 15:7 when one of them unleashes the last seven plagues of God's wrath on mankind.

The four living creatures are similar to the cherubim described in Ezekiel chapters 1 and 10. In both Ezekiel 1 and Revelation 4, the number of the creatures is four. They are "covered with eyes" (Revelation 4:6; cf. Ezekiel 1:18; 10:12). They have faces appearing like those of a man, a lion, an ox, and an eagle (Ezekiel 1:10–11; cf. Revelation 4:7).

At the same time, the living creatures in Revelation 4 are similar to the seraphim described in Isaiah 6. They have six wings (Revelation 4:8; cf. Isaiah 6:2), and their words of praise emphasize God's holiness (Revelation 4:8; cf. Isaiah 6:3).

In summary, the living creatures of Revelation 4 are an exalted order of angels whose purpose is primarily to worship the Lord

(Revelation 19:4). They are similar to the beings in Ezekiel 1 and 10 and Isaiah 6:1–3, and they are somehow involved in God's divine justice.

32. Who are the watcher angels/Grigori?

The term *Grigori* is not found in Scripture. But watcher angels are mentioned in three verses of the Bible, each in a vision that King Nebuchadnezzar had (Daniel 4:13, 17, 23). Not all translations use the term *watcher angels*. The ESV and KJV speak of "a watcher" in Daniel 4:13, and the NASB calls it "an angelic watcher," but the NIV simply calls this being "a messenger" from heaven. The NET says that Nebuchadnezzar sees "a holy sentinel." These watcher angels are supernatural, celestial beings, or "holy ones," who come down from heaven with authority to speak for God.

In Daniel 4, the word translated "watcher" comes from a Hebrew root meaning "wakeful one," which is why it is often translated as "watcher." The *Topical Encyclopedia* associates watcher angels with a heavenly council who "serve as intermediaries between God and humanity, tasked with observing human actions and implementing divine judgments."[3]

Noncanonical literature elaborates in detail regarding the watcher angels. According to the books of Enoch, watcher angels can be either fallen angels or holy angels. These watcher angels take a particular interest in the earthly affairs of human beings, "watching" them, and, at times, even interfering in or controlling situations that concern people. The fall of the watcher angels unfolds in the apocryphal book of 1 Enoch. Part of Enoch's mission is to pronounce God's judgment on the fallen watcher angels who supposedly dwelled in the fifth heaven where their fall took place.

Grigori is the name Enoch assigns to these fallen watcher angels in the book of 2 Enoch. The English word *Grigori* is simply a transliteration of the Greek word for "watcher" used in the Septuagint.

According to the account in 2 Enoch, the watcher angels are sent down to earth to look after humans. They soon develop an unnatural lust for the beautiful women of earth. A group of rebellious watchers, the Grigori, seduce the women of earth and impregnate them with a race of hybrid giants who violently raid the earth and threaten humanity.

Another noncanonical book, Jubilees, also speaks of heavenly watchers who violate their ordained nature by lusting after and having sexual relations with human women. According to Jubilees, the offspring of their unnatural unions are monstrous giants who corrupt the children of earth and prompt the flood of Noah's time.

These extrabiblical writings seem to provide an explanation for the creatures mentioned in Genesis 6:1–4 called Nephilim. The Bible tells us that Nephilim were the result of sexual relations between "the sons of God" and "the daughters of humans" (Genesis 6:2). Much debate exists regarding the identity and origin of the Nephilim. The only solid information we can gather from Scripture is that the Nephilim are the offspring of the sons of God and human women and are described as "heroes of old" and "men of renown" (v. 4). Numbers 13:33 suggests that the Nephilim were a people of extraordinary size, possibly associating them with giants.

Substantial debate also surrounds the nature of the "sons of God" who fathered the Nephilim. Were they fallen watcher angels, or Grigori? Does the biblical book of Jude provide a clue? "And the angels who did not keep their positions of authority but abandoned their proper dwelling—these he has kept in darkness, bound with everlasting chains for judgment on the great Day" (Jude 1:6). For now, we can only speculate. The Bible does not provide us with clear answers; therefore, we must be content with uncertainty.

We are wise to be extra cautious about giving serious weight to the ideas found in extrabiblical sources. Nevertheless, Scripture does affirm the concept of heavenly beings who watch the earth and are interested in the affairs of humans: "This Good News has been announced to you by those who preached in the power of the

Holy Spirit sent from heaven. It is all so wonderful that even the angels are eagerly watching these things happen" (1 Peter 1:12 NLT).

Since God's purpose is to use the church to display His wisdom to rulers and authorities in the heavenly realms (Ephesians 3:10), then the idea of attentive watcher angels or guardians is biblically sound. Likewise, the Bible confirms the presence of angels who guard and protect humans: "The angel of the LORD encamps around those who fear him, and he delivers them" (Psalm 34:7; see also Matthew 18:10; Acts 12:9–15).

33. Who is the destroying angel?

The destroying angel is also commonly referred to as the angel of death. On numerous occasions, God used angelic beings—heavenly messengers of some kind—to bring judgment to sinners on earth. Various Bible translations refer to this being as a "destroying angel." There is no clear biblical evidence that any one particular angel was given the title "destroying angel" or "angel of death." The most we can say is that the Bible's mentions of a "destroying angel" are references to a heavenly being or beings that came to destroy those under God's judgment.

A possible visitation of a destroying angel was on the first Passover. Egypt was about to experience the tenth and final plague, the death of the firstborn. Moses' instructions to the Hebrews contained this warning: "When the LORD goes through the land to strike down the Egyptians, he will see the blood on the top and sides of the doorframe and will pass over that doorway, and he will not permit the destroyer to enter your houses and strike you down" (Exodus 12:23). Some other translations have "Angel of Death" (GNT) or "death angel" (NLT) instead of "destroyer." This being is called "the destroyer of the firstborn" in Hebrews 11:28.

Interestingly, the original Hebrew text of Exodus 12:23 does not mention an "angel" at all. It simply says that "the destroyer" or "the spoiler" or "the one who causes damage" would slay the first-born of Egypt. It could have been the Lord Himself who was the destroyer. Psalm 78 recounts the plagues in Egypt and sums them up as God's unleashing of "a band of destroying angels" (v. 49). The Hebrew word for "angel" is used here, but the form is plural and so is not limited to one particular angel.

A destroying angel—a heavenly messenger who brought destruction—was also sent by God to judge the Israelites because of David's sin in numbering the people:

> The LORD sent a plague on Israel from that morning until the end of the time designated, and seventy thousand of the people from Dan to Beersheba died. When the angel stretched out his hand to destroy Jerusalem, the LORD relented concerning the disaster and said to the angel who was afflicting the people, "Enough! Withdraw your hand." The angel of the LORD was then at the threshing floor of Araunah the Jebusite.
>
> When David saw the angel who was striking down the people, he said to the LORD, "I have sinned."
>
> 2 Samuel 24:15–17

The Assyrians who attacked Jerusalem during King Hezekiah's reign also met what could be called an angel of death or a destroying angel: "That night the angel of the LORD went out and put to death a hundred and eighty-five thousand in the Assyrian camp. When the people got up the next morning—there were all the dead bodies!" (2 Kings 19:35). In this passage and in 2 Samuel 24, the destroying angel is actually called "the angel of the LORD," which many scholars take to be a reference to Christ in a preincarnate appearance.

Another angel who brought death and destruction is mentioned in the judgment of King Herod (Acts 12:23). An angel with lethal intent, identified as "the angel of the LORD," bears a sword as he gives a warning to Balaam (Numbers 22:31–33). And Jesus mentions that angels will be involved in the end-times judgment of the wicked (Matthew 13:49–50). In none of these cases are the angels called "the angel of destruction" or "the angel of death." We might refer to an angel who metes out God's judgment as an "angel of destruction," but it is not an explicitly biblical term.

34. Do we have guardian angels?

In Matthew 18:10 Jesus states, "See that you do not look down on one of these little ones; for I say to you that their angels in heaven continually see the face of My Father who is in heaven" (NASB). In this context, "these little ones" could either apply to people who believe in Him (v. 6) or to little children (vv. 3–5). Jesus' reference to "their angels" makes this the key passage giving rise to the idea of guardian angels.

There is no doubt that good angels help protect (Daniel 6:20–23; 2 Kings 6:13–17), reveal information to (Acts 7:52–53; Luke 1:11–20), guide (Matthew 1:20–21; Acts 8:26), provide for (Genesis 21:17–20; 1 Kings 19:5–7), and minister to believers in general (Hebrews 1:14). The question is whether each person—or each believer—has an angel assigned to him or her. Do we all have an angel who acts as our personal "guardian"?

In the Old Testament, the archangel Michael is called "the great prince who protects [Daniel's] people" (Daniel 12:1; cf. 10:21). So, it would seem that nations may have a "guardian angel." But Scripture nowhere states that an angel is assigned to an individual for oversight or guardianship. Some early church fathers such as Origen believed that each person had not only a good angel assigned to him or her, but a demon as well.[4]

The word *their* in Matthew 18:10 is a collective pronoun in the Greek. Do not despise the little ones, Jesus said, because "their" angels are "always" watching the face of God—the idea is that the angels wait attentively to hear God's command and carry out His wishes regarding people. The angels in this passage do not seem to be guarding a person so much as being attentive to the Father in heaven. The active duty or oversight, then, comes from God rather than from angels. God alone is omniscient, and He alone knows when one of us needs the intervention of an angel. The angels stand ready to serve and help one of God's "little ones."

The question of whether we have guardian angels assigned to us cannot be emphatically answered from Scripture. God does use angels in ministering to us. What that ministry entails is open to speculation. In the end, we know that our omniscient, omnipotent, all-loving God is mindful of us. We can praise Him as David did:

> You know when I sit and when I rise;
>   you perceive my thoughts from afar.
> You discern my going out and my lying down;
>   you are familiar with all my ways.
> Before a word is on my tongue
>   you, LORD, know it completely.
> You hem me in behind and before,
>   and you lay your hand upon me.
>
> Psalm 139:2–5

35. Who is the angel of the Lord?

The precise identity of the angel of the Lord is not given in the Bible; however, there are many important clues that indicate the angel of the Lord is a unique being, separate from the other angels. Here are some instances of the angel of the Lord showing up in Scripture:

- He finds Hagar in the wilderness and gives her a promise concerning her son, Ishmael (Genesis 16:7–12; cf. 21:17–18).

- He stops Abraham from sacrificing Isaac (Genesis 22:11–18).
- He appears to Moses "in flames of fire from within a bush" (Exodus 3:2).
- He delivers a message to wayward Israel (Judges 2:1–4).
- He commissions Gideon and performs a miracle for him (Judges 6:11–24).
- He brings a plague on Israel during David's time (2 Samuel 24:15–17).
- He appears in a vision of the prophet Zechariah (Zechariah 1:11–13; cf. 3:1–10).

In various passages, the angel of the Lord speaks as God, identifies Himself with God, and exercises the responsibilities of God. In several of these appearances, those who saw the angel of the Lord feared for their lives because they had "seen God" (Judges 13:22; cf. Judges 6:22). Therefore, we can say that, in at least some instances, the angel of the Lord is a theophany, an appearance of God in physical form.

The appearances of the angel of the Lord cease after the incarnation of Christ. Angels are mentioned numerous times in the New Testament, but "the angel of the Lord" is never mentioned in the New Testament after the birth of Christ. One possible difficulty is that the angel who appears to Joseph in a dream in Matthew 1:24 is called "the" angel of the Lord. However, this angel is clearly the same one appearing in verse 20, which calls him "an" angel. Matthew is simply referencing the same angel he had just mentioned. There is also some confusion regarding Matthew 28:2, where the KJV says "the angel of the Lord" descended from heaven and rolled the stone away from Jesus' tomb. Here, it is important to note that the original Greek has no article in front of the word for "angel"; it could be "the angel" or "an angel," but the article must be supplied by the translators.

Other translations besides the KJV say it was "an angel," which is the better wording.

It is possible that appearances of the angel of the Lord represent the Son of God taking on temporary human form—a preincarnate appearance of Jesus Christ. Jesus declared Himself to be existent "before Abraham" (John 8:58), so it makes sense that He would be active and could manifest in the world. Whatever the case, whether the angel of the Lord was a preincarnate appearance of Christ (a Christophany) or an appearance of God the Father (a theophany), it is likely that "the angel of the Lord" was, in most cases, a physical appearance of God.

SECTION 5

Questions About Us and Angels

36. Do we become angels after we die?

Angels are spirit beings created by God (Colossians 1:15–17) and are entirely different from humans. They are God's special agents to carry out His plan and to minister to the followers of Christ (Hebrews 1:13–14). There is no indication that angels were formerly humans or anything else—they were created as angels.

One difference between angels and humans is that angels have no need of, and cannot experience, the redemption that Christ offers the human race. First Peter 1:12 says the angels "long to look into" the things concerning salvation. Had they formerly been humans, angels would not find salvation mysterious. Angels are curious about God's plan, and they rejoice whenever a sinner turns to Christ (Luke 15:10), but forgiveness of sin and the gift of salvation are not part of their personal experience.

When a believer dies, his or her spirit goes to be with Christ (2 Corinthians 5:8) to be reunited with the body at the resurrection (1 Thessalonians 4:16). The believer does not become an angel in heaven. When Elijah and Moses appeared on the Mount of Transfiguration, they had not transformed into angels; they appeared as themselves—although glorified—and were recognizable to Peter, James, and John (Matthew 17:1–3).

One passage that some people misconstrue to mean we become angels when we die is Matthew 22:30. Jesus, in answering a question from the Sadducees, said, "At the resurrection people will neither marry nor be given in marriage; they will be like the angels in heaven." But Jesus was not teaching that we *become* angels, only that we will be *like* the angels in one respect: We will not marry in the eternal state. Angels do not marry, and, after the resurrection, neither will we.

God redeems us body, soul, and spirit, and we will live with the Lord forever. He made us human, and we will remain human throughout eternity. Angels remain angels. All serve and worship God our Creator, saying, "Amen! Praise and glory and wisdom and thanks and honor and power and strength be to our God for ever and ever. Amen!" (Revelation 7:12).

37. Do Christians have the authority to command angels?

People are fascinated by the concept and study of angels, formally called "angelology." Depictions of angels are found everywhere—in jewelry, digital art, wall hangings, movies, and of course, Christmas decorations. Just as ubiquitous are the misconceptions about angels. Some Christians, for example, believe they have the authority to command angels to do their bidding. Others believe their authority extends even to the demons.

There are no instances in Scripture where humans were able to give angels commands, either in their own name or in Jesus' name. There are no passages in which man has control over the work that angels do. On the contrary, Scripture teaches that mankind was created "a little lower than the angels" (Psalm 8:5; cf. Hebrews 2:7–9). Angels outrank us.

The teaching that believers have control over angels is false. Scripture teaches that angels listen to and obey God: "Praise the LORD, you his angels, you mighty ones who do his bidding, who obey his word" (Psalm 103:20). The following biblical examples help show that angels are not subject to the commands of men:

- Moses reminded the children of Israel, "When we cried out to the LORD, he heard our cry and sent an angel and brought us out of Egypt" (Numbers 20:16). The Israelites did not command an angel to come to them. They appealed to God, under whose command the angels function.
- Shadrach, Meshach, and Abednego refused to bow down to Nebuchadnezzar's image (Daniel 3:17–18). God in His mercy "sent his angel and rescued his servants!" (Daniel 3:28). The three godly Hebrews did not summon the angel of the Lord. God sent him. God later "sent his angel" to deliver Daniel from the lions (Daniel 6:22). No one but God is commanding the angels to do anything.
- The church in Jerusalem prayed for Peter when he was in prison (Acts 12:5). When Peter was delivered, he testified, "Now I know without a doubt that the Lord has sent his angel and rescued me from Herod's clutches" (Acts 12:11). The Christians praying for Peter were so surprised when he came to their door that they almost did not let him in. Certainly, they had not commanded any angel to perform the rescue.

It's true that Paul, in Acts 16:18, commands an evil spirit to come out of a girl "in the name of Jesus Christ," and the demon obeys. This is an example of apostolic authority. The Twelve had been specifically commissioned by Jesus to carry His message and demonstrate His power (see Acts 3:6–8). The apostles' casting out of demons has no bearing on believers today ordering angels around.

Jesus calls the holy angels "angels of God" in Luke 12:8. God is the owner of the angels; they belong to Him. Angels do God's bidding, not ours.

38. What does it mean that we should entertain strangers because we might entertain angels (Hebrews 13:2)?

The writer of Hebrews urges believers to show hospitality by offering an extraordinary incentive: "Do not forget to entertain strangers, for by so doing some have unwittingly entertained angels" (Hebrews 13:2 NKJV). The encouragement is part of a more extensive teaching on showing brotherly love to fellow Christians.

Demonstrating brotherly love means treating fellow Christians as we would beloved family members. One way believers can do this is by pitching in to care for the needs of Christian ministers and missionaries, showing hospitality, and entertaining them in our homes.

First-century accommodations for travelers were often unavailable, especially in smaller towns. If lodgings existed, they were typically expensive, immoral, and unsanitary establishments. It was much more common for travelers to stay in the home of a friend or family member.

In the New Living Translation, Hebrews 13:2 says, "Don't forget to show hospitality to strangers, for some who have done this have entertained angels without realizing it!" This passage makes direct reference to Genesis 18–19, when both Abraham and Lot showed hospitality to mysterious visitors who, in reality, were messengers sent by God. Abraham and Lot literally entertained angels. The author of Hebrews conveys this principle: It is preferable to open our homes to needy guests than run the risk of offending God by treating His messengers inhospitably.

God's servants who travel about as missionaries and ministers give more blessings than they receive. Therefore, believers should be generous in supporting them and helping them accomplish their work (1 Corinthians 9:11–14; 16:17). The apostle Paul instructed the Galatians, "Those who are taught the word of God should provide for their teachers, sharing all good things with them" (Galatians 6:6 NLT). Paul explained to Timothy that one of the qualities required of a church leader is, "He must enjoy having guests in his home" (1 Timothy 3:2 NLT).

Jesus also upheld the principle of entertaining strangers. He said that whenever we refuse to help a servant of the Lord—the needy, the stranger, the hungry, the thirsty, the sick, and "the least of these my brothers and sisters"—we are refusing to help the Lord Himself (Matthew 25:35–45). When we entertain strangers, we are showing hospitality to Jesus Christ our Lord and demonstrating brotherly love.

True brotherly love is not satisfied with mere words but expresses itself with deeds of compassion. Opening our homes to visitors and being generous with our possessions is how we prove our love for one another and faithfulness to God:

> Dear friend, you are being faithful to God when you care for the traveling teachers who pass through, even though they are strangers to you. They have told the church here of your loving friendship. Please continue providing for such teachers in a manner that pleases God. For they are traveling for the Lord, and they accept nothing from people who are not believers. So we ourselves should support them so that we can be their partners as they teach the truth.
>
> 3 John 1:5–8 NLT

Today, we can look for opportunities to "entertain strangers" by accommodating traveling ministers and missionaries, inviting fellow Christians into our homes for a meal, or hosting an informal life group, prayer meeting, or Bible study.

"When God's people are in need, be ready to help them. Always be eager to practice hospitality," urged Paul (Romans 12:13 NLT). We may never know if, by welcoming a stranger, we somehow entertained an angel of the Lord. But we can be sure that, by showing warm, generous hospitality to our brothers and sisters in Christ, we are being faithful and obedient to the Lord's will.

39. Does the Bible promote or prohibit praying to angels?

There is no verse that explicitly states, "You shall not pray to angels"; at the same time, praying to angels violates the Bible's clear teaching on prayer and ignores the role angels play. Prayer is an act of worship. The holy angels, being fellow servants of ours, reject our worship (Revelation 22:8–9), so they would also reject our prayers. Offering our worship or prayer to anyone but God is idolatry.

Jesus Christ never prayed to anyone but the Father. When instructing His disciples to pray, He started with, "Our Father in heaven" (Matthew 6:9; cf. John 16:23). If praying to angels were appropriate, He would have modeled such a prayer for us. But Jesus addressed all of His prayers to the heavenly Father (e.g., Matthew 11:25; John 11:41; 17:1). Further, the content of Jesus' prayers usually involved requests for assistance that could only be granted by someone who is omnipotent, omniscient, and omnipresent—i.e., God.

In His High Priestly Prayer, Jesus prays on behalf of His followers, requesting their sanctification, glorification, and preservation (John 17:1–26). These three blessings can only come from the

One who has the power to grant them. Angels cannot sanctify us, they cannot glorify us, and they cannot guarantee our inheritance in Christ (Ephesians 1:13–14).

In John 14:13–14, Christ tells believers that, whatever we ask in His name, He will accomplish because He pleads directly with the Father. Offering a prayer to angels falls short of an effective and biblically guided prayer. In John 16:26–27, Jesus says that "in that day you will ask in my name" and that the Father will hear because "the Father himself loves you."

Jesus Christ is the one and only intercessor between the Father and believers (1 Timothy 2:5). Neither angels nor any other created being is ever depicted in the Bible as our intercessor. We pray to the Father in the name of the Son and in the power of the Holy Spirit. Why pray to angels, who have no power to mediate on our behalf?

First Thessalonians 5:17 tells the believer to pray without ceasing. Angels are finite beings and not capable of hearing incessant prayer. God is infinite—He is always present and available to listen to the pleas of every person all the time. God can answer prayer through the agency of an angel (see Daniel 9:20–23), but the angel has no power in himself to receive and answer our prayers.

40. Is it wrong to have angel figurines?

Having an angel figurine or displaying a depiction of an angel in artwork is not inherently wrong. In fact, placing an angel atop a Christmas tree can be a wonderful token of the role angels played in announcing the birth of Christ. Wearing an angel lapel pin could be a reminder of God's provision and constant care.

Having angel figurines could be wrong in some circumstances. If, for example, a person idolizes the figurines, prays to them, worships them, or considers them "good luck," then the figurines are being used for ungodly purposes. We pray to God and worship only Him (Psalm 99:5; Luke 4:8). We reject superstition and keep ourselves from idols (1 John 5:21). We rely fully on God alone (Psalm 9:10). Christians must be careful never to allow religious imagery, whether an angel figurine, a picture of Jesus, a cross pendant, etc., to become a snare or distraction.

No figurine, of an angel or anything else, has any supernatural power or influence over our lives. An angel figurine cannot protect us from harm, bring us good luck, or impact us in any way. Such beliefs are mere superstition, which has no place in the life of a Christian. Physical objects do not have magical powers. "Don't let anyone capture you with . . . high-sounding nonsense that come[s] from human thinking and from the spiritual powers of this world, rather than from Christ. For in Christ lives all the fullness of God in a human body. So you also are complete through your union with Christ" (Colossians 2:8–10 NLT).

In addition to all that has been said, we do not know what actual angels look like. Even at their best, angel figurines are only someone's idea of what angels might look like.

SECTION 6
Questions About Demons

41. What does the Bible say about demons?

Demons are fallen angels, as Revelation 12:9 indicates: "The great dragon was hurled down—that ancient serpent called the devil, or Satan, who leads the whole world astray. He was hurled to the earth, and his angels with him." Satan's fall from heaven is symbolically described in Isaiah 14:12–15 and Ezekiel 28:12–15. When he fell, Satan took some of the angels with him—one third of them, according to Revelation 12:4. Jude 1:6 also mentions angels who sinned. So, biblically, demons are fallen angels who, along with Satan, chose to rebel against God.

Some of the demons are already locked "in darkness, bound with everlasting chains" (Jude 1:6) for their sin. Others are free to roam and are referred to as "the powers of this dark world and

. . . the spiritual forces of evil in the heavenly realms" in Ephesians 6:12 (cf. Colossians 2:15). The demons still follow Satan as their leader and do battle with the holy angels in an attempt to thwart God's plan and hinder God's people (Daniel 10:13).

Demons, as spirit beings, have the ability to take possession of a physical body. Demonic possession occurs when a person's body is completely controlled by a demon. This cannot happen to a child of God, since the Holy Spirit resides in the heart of the believer in Christ (1 John 4:4).

Jesus, during His earthly ministry, encountered many demons. Of course, none of them were a match for the power of Christ: "Many who were demon-possessed were brought to him, and he drove out the spirits with a word" (Matthew 8:16). Jesus' authority over the demons was one of the proofs that He was indeed the Son of God (Luke 11:20). The demons who encountered Jesus knew who He was, and they feared Him: "'What do you want with us, Son of God?' [the demons] shouted. 'Have you come here to torture us before the appointed time?'" (Matthew 8:29). The demons know their end will be one of torment.

Satan and his demons now look to destroy the work of God and deceive anyone they can (1 Peter 5:8; 2 Corinthians 11:14–15). The demons are described in most translations as evil, unclean, or impure spirits (Matthew 10:1; Mark 1:27), lying or deceiving spirits (1 Kings 22:23), and angels of Satan (Revelation 12:9). Satan and his demons deceive the world (2 Corinthians 4:4), promulgate false doctrine (1 Timothy 4:1), attack Christians (2 Corinthians 12:7; 1 Peter 5:8), and combat the holy angels (Revelation 12:4–9).

The demons/fallen angels are enemies of God, but they are defeated enemies. Christ has "disarmed the powers and authorities," and He has "made a public spectacle of them, triumphing over them by the cross" (Colossians 2:15). As we submit to God and resist the devil, we have nothing to fear. "The one who is in you is greater than the one who is in the world" (1 John 4:4).

42. Did one third of the angels fall with Lucifer?

There is no verse in the Bible that says, "A third of the angels fell from heaven." The idea that, when Satan rebelled against God, one third of the angels went with him comes from certain other verses that, when put together, suggest that's what happened.

On the sixth day of creation, God declared everything to be "very good" (Genesis 1:31). We assume the "everything" includes angels. Sometime after that, Satan rebelled against God and was cast out of heaven. Jesus witnessed the event: "I saw Satan fall like lightning from heaven" (Luke 10:18)—an event that the Lord uses to explain the exorcisms performed by the seventy-two disciples (v. 17).

Another passage that also seems to describe the fall of Satan from heaven is Isaiah 14:12–15. The context is primarily about a human king, as judgment is pronounced against Babylon. The poetic language used by Isaiah is so grand, however, that many scholars have concluded that there is more to the passage. References to "the whole earth" (Isaiah 14:7 NKJV), the king's having "fallen from heaven" (v. 12), his desire to exalt himself "above the stars" (v. 13), and the symbolic name *Lucifer* or *Light-bringer* (v. 12 NKJV) are all expressions of hyperbolic greatness. If the intended subject is *only* the human king of Babylon, then everything is figurative (and greatly exaggerated); however, if there is a secondary spiritual character in view, then the descriptions could be quite literal. God is pronouncing judgment on *both* "kings of Babylon"—the human king and the spiritual potentate who empowers him (*Babylon* being a symbol of rebellion from Genesis to Revelation). The wonderment of Isaiah 14:12 ("How you have fallen from heaven, morning star, son of the dawn! You have been cast down to the earth, you who once laid low the nations!") could indeed have a dual interpretation.

Further, the book of Revelation describes "a star that had fallen from the sky to the earth" (Revelation 9:1). This "star" is given a key to the bottomless pit and proceeds to release a horde of tormenting "locusts" (Revelation 9:2–11). While Revelation 9:1 is not a clear reference to Satan, it *could* be: The fact that the "star" that fell from heaven has a key (authority) is no problem, especially since he uses the key to unleash terror upon the earth.

So, the Bible explicitly and implicitly teaches that Satan fell from his position in heaven. But how do we know that one third of the angels also fell with him?

The passage that best supports the idea that Satan took one third of the angels with him in rebellion is Revelation 12:3–4. John sees a sign in heaven: "An enormous red dragon with seven heads and ten horns and seven crowns on its heads. Its tail swept a third of the stars out of the sky and flung them to the earth." John then relates that the dragon was hurled down to the earth and positively identifies it as "that ancient serpent called the devil, or Satan, who leads the whole world astray" (Revelation 12:9). The dragon is not thrown to earth alone, however: "His angels were cast out with him" (Revelation 12:9 NKJV). The angels that are ejected from heaven with Satan we associate with the "third of the stars" that the dragon's tail swept from heaven to earth in verse 4.

If the "stars" of Revelation 12:4 are indeed a symbolic reference to Satan's "angels" in verse 9, then what we have is a reference to the fall of a portion of the angels (the heavenly hosts) who followed Satan in his rebellion. Two thirds of the angels remained loyal to God and are called the "holy angels" in Scripture (e.g., Mark 8:38); one third of the original angels joined Satan and are called "unclean spirits" or "demons" today (e.g., Mark 9:25).

43. Are demons fallen angels?

When exactly God created angels is open for debate, but what is known for sure is that God created everything good (Genesis

1:31). God, in His holiness, cannot create something sinful. So, when Satan, who was once the angel Lucifer, rebelled against God, he lost his position in heaven (Isaiah 14; Ezekiel 28). One third of the angelic host joined his insurrection (Revelation 12:3–4, 9). It is likely that these fallen angels are now known as the demons.

Hell was prepared for the devil and his angels, according to Matthew 25:41: "Then [the Lord] will say to those on his left, 'Depart from me, you who are cursed, into the eternal fire prepared for the devil and his angels.'" The possessive pronoun *his* indicates that these angels belong to Satan. Revelation 12:7–9 describes an end-times angelic battle between Michael and "his angels" and the devil and "his angels." From these and similar verses, it seems that demons and fallen angels are synonymous.

Some reject the idea that the demons are the fallen angels, citing Jude 1:6, which says the angels who sinned are "bound with everlasting chains." However, not *all* of the sinful angels are bound, as Satan is still free (1 Peter 5:8). Why would God imprison all the fallen angels except for the leader of the rebellion? It seems likely that the confined angels took part in a more heinous rebellion—likely the "sons of God" incident in Genesis chapter 6.

An alternate explanation for the origin of the demons is that they are the spirits of the Nephilim destroyed in the flood (Genesis 6). According to this view, the unclean spirits who repeatedly confronted Jesus (e.g., Mark 3:11, ESV) were the disembodied souls of half-human, half-angelic beings who lived before the flood. The Bible does not say what happened to the souls of the Nephilim when the flood swept them away, so it's *possible* that they were allowed to remain on earth in an incorporeal state. We believe the most biblically consistent explanation for the origin of the demons is that they are the fallen angels who continue their satanic rebellion against God.

44. What are evil spirits?

Evil spirits are referred to in both the Old and New Testaments but are often called by other names such as "unclean [or impure] spirits," "deceiving [or lying] spirits," "demonic spirits," and "demons." In all cases, evil spirits are malevolent supernatural beings. Evil spirits work against God, but God in His sovereignty can choose to use evil spirits to carry out His plans and purposes, demonstrating that He is Ruler over all the universe.

The Bible does not reveal the origin of evil spirits. They are most likely angels who fell with Satan at his rebellion (Matthew 25:41; Revelation 12:7–9). Evil spirits function as part of the hierarchy of evil (Ephesians 6:12), with Satan as their leader (Matthew 12:24).

Most of the evil spirits mentioned in the Old Testament were sent from God as a punishment on disobedient humans (1 Kings 22:20–23). In Judges 9:23, an evil spirit was used by God to judge Abimelech and avenge the murder of Gideon's sons. God is not the author of evil, but He can allow evil powers, subject to His control, to bring about certain consequences in accordance with His plan.

The Lord sent an evil spirit to show that He had rejected Saul as king. The evil spirit caused Saul to experience fits of temper and despair: "Now the Spirit of the LORD had left Saul, and the LORD sent a tormenting spirit that filled him with depression and fear. Some of Saul's servants said to him, 'A tormenting spirit from God is troubling you'" (1 Samuel 16:14–15 NLT).

In the New Testament, the term *demon* is often used interchangeably with *evil spirit*. These wicked entities defile and bring evil to human subjects. Their intention may be to inflict physical harm, disability, and sickness rather than moral corruption.

Evil spirits can possess people, and Jesus Christ several times cast out evil spirits (Matthew 8:16; Mark 5:1–13; 7:24–30). He gave His disciples power to do the same in His name (Matthew

10:1; Acts 5:12–16; 8:4–8). Evil spirits know who Jesus is and that He will judge and condemn them in the future (Matthew 8:29; Mark 1:24; 5:7).

In the end times, many people will be deceived by evil spirits and the false teachings they inspire (1 Timothy 4:1). The book of Revelation speaks of deceptive evil spirits playing a significant role in the last days:

> And I saw three evil spirits that looked like frogs leap from the mouths of the dragon, the beast, and the false prophet. They are demonic spirits who work miracles and go out to all the rulers of the world to gather them for battle against the Lord on that great judgment day of God the Almighty.
>
> > "Look, I will come as unexpectedly as a thief! Blessed are all who are watching for me, who keep their clothing ready so they will not have to walk around naked and ashamed."
>
> And the demonic spirits gathered all the rulers and their armies to a place with the Hebrew name Armageddon.
>
> Revelation 16:13–16 NLT

Evil spirits are part of Satan's dark forces, enemies of God and His people. Evil spirits promote corruption, malice, and depravity in the world and in individual lives. They are opposed to God's holiness, goodness, righteousness, light, and love. As the antithesis of the Holy Spirit, evil spirits represent the opposite of God's character, nature, and will. They are hostile to the work of God and Jesus Christ, and believers are always to resist them: "Be alert and of sober mind. Your enemy the devil prowls around like a roaring lion looking for someone to devour. Resist him, standing firm in the faith" (1 Peter 5:8–9; see also Ephesians 6:13; James 4:7).

45. What are unclean spirits?

Unclean spirit is simply a New Testament synonym and more descriptive Jewish term for *demon*. The terms *unclean spirit* and *demon* seem to be interchangeable in Scripture. Some translations, including the NIV, refer to them as "impure spirits."

Throughout the New Testament, the term *unclean spirits* (*akathartos* in the Greek language) is mentioned over twenty times. In various passages we read that unclean spirits can possess people and cause them sickness and harm (Matthew 10:1; 12:43; Mark 1:26; Luke 4:36; 6:18; Acts 5:16; 8:7); they are searching for someone to possess (Matthew 12:43); some are more unclean than others (Luke 11:26); unclean spirits can interact with one another (Mark 5:1–20; Matthew 12:45); and unclean spirits are under God's authority and must submit to Him (Mark 1:27; 3:11; 5:8, 13).

An unclean spirit or demon is "unclean" in that it is wicked. Evil spirits are not only wicked themselves, but they delight in wickedness and promote sinfulness in humans. They are spiritually polluted, and they seek to contaminate all of God's creation with their filth. Their foul nature is in direct contrast to the purity and incorruption of the Holy Spirit's nature. When a person is defiled by an unclean spirit, he takes pleasure in corrupt thoughts and actions; when a person is filled with the Holy Spirit, his thoughts and actions are heavenly.

Some people hold the idea that unclean spirits or demons are deceased humans who may or may not have been evil while alive. However, we infer that the unclean spirits mentioned in the Bible are not referring to the dead for several reasons. One, humans are never called "spirits" when the word *spirit* is used as a standalone term, without a possessive. In Scripture, men are said to have a spirit/soul (saying "his spirit" in Proverbs 25:28 NKJV and 1 Corinthians 5:5), but men are not called "spirits." Two, once a person dies, he or she immediately enters either eternal life with the Lord or eternal darkness in hell (Hebrews 9:27; 2 Corinthians 5:6–8; Matthew 25:46). Human spirits do not and cannot wander on earth in their spirit bodies.

A related theory is that unclean spirits are the departed spirits of the Nephilim who were killed in the flood of Noah's day. This view could have some validity, but our opinion is that unclean spirits or demons are fallen angels. Demons are unclean, unholy, impure, and evil, and they are doomed to an eternity in hell (Matthew 25:41).

46. What are principalities and powers?

The phrase *principalities and powers* occurs six times in the Bible, always in the King James Version and its derivatives (the New King James Version and the Modern King James Version). Other versions translate it variously as "rulers and authorities," "forces and authorities," and "rulers and powers." In most places where the phrase appears, the reference is to the vast array of evil and malicious spirits who make war against the people of God. The principalities and powers are satanic—they are spiritual beings that wield power in the unseen realms to oppose everything and everyone that is of God.

The first mention of principalities and powers is in Romans 8:37–39: "Yet in all these things we are more than conquerors through Him who loved us. For I am persuaded that neither death nor life, nor angels nor principalities nor powers, nor things present nor things to come, nor height nor depth, nor any other created thing, shall be able to separate us from the love of God which is in Christ Jesus our Lord" (NKJV). These verses are about the victory Christ has won over all the forces ranged against us. We are "more than conquerors" because no force—not life, not death, not angels, not demons, indeed nothing—can separate us from the love of God. The "powers" referred to here are those with miraculous powers, whether false teachers and prophets or the demonic entities that empower them. Whatever their power, they cannot separate us from the love of God. Our victory is assured.

Another mention of principalities and powers is in Colossians 1:16, “For by Him all things were created that are in heaven and that are on earth, visible and invisible, whether thrones or dominions or principalities or powers. All things were created through Him and for Him” (NKJV). The Son of God is the Creator and Ruler over all authorities, whether they submit to Him or rebel against Him. The forces of evil are subject to the control of our sovereign Lord, who uses even the wicked for bringing about His perfect plan and purpose (Daniel 4:35; Isaiah 46:10–11).

Colossians 2:15 pinpoints the moment of Jesus’ triumph as His substitutionary atonement on the cross: “Having disarmed principalities and powers, He made a public spectacle of them, triumphing over them in [the cross]” (NKJV). The principalities and powers are not to be feared, for they have been disarmed at the cross. Satan and his legions had drawn mankind into captivity, subjecting them to their evil reign. But Christ, by His death, subdued the enemy and “rescued us from the dominion of darkness” (Colossians 1:13).

Ephesians 3:10–11 speaks of a broader set of principalities and powers—the holy and unholy angels in the heavenly realms: “To the intent that now the manifold wisdom of God might be made known by the church to the principalities and powers in the heavenly places, according to the eternal purpose which He accomplished in Christ Jesus our Lord” (NKJV). The wisdom and purpose of God in the plan of salvation shine through the church. Angels now witness the glory of God and the preeminence of Christ, as God has redeemed a people for Himself and preserves them by His power (Ephesians 1:20–21).

Ephesians 6:12 specifies that we battle “against principalities, against powers, against the rulers of the darkness of this age, against spiritual hosts of wickedness in the heavenly places” (NKJV). We have been given spiritual armor to fight the fight (Ephesians 6:13–18). We "stand firm" (Ephesians 6:11 NLT), knowing our enemy has been disarmed—the serpent has been defanged, and victory is promised.

The final reference to principalities and powers is Titus 3:1, where believers are admonished to "be subject to principalities and powers" (KJV). In this context, the rulers are those governmental authorities whom God has placed over us for our protection and welfare. Submission to God involves submission to His duly constituted human authorities. Those who rebel against earthly authorities are "rebelling against what God has instituted, and those who do so will bring judgment on themselves" (Romans 13:2).

47. How are idols connected to demons (Deuteronomy 32:16–17)?

Deuteronomy 32:16–17 states, "They stirred him to jealousy with strange gods; with abominations they provoked him to anger. They sacrificed to demons that were not God, to gods they had never known, to new gods that had come recently, whom your fathers had never dreaded" (ESV). This passage associates pagan gods with "demons" and warns God's people not to be involved with idolatry.

The Hebrew text here uses synonymous parallelism, in which two or more lines communicate the same idea using different words. In this case, the parallels include the following:

strange gods
abominations
demons that were not God
new gods

Grammatically, the "demons" and the "strange (foreign) gods" are the same. The text directly connects pagan worship with evil spirits. The false gods are contrasted with the true God, the "Rock" that created and saved the Israelites in verses 15 and 17.

Leviticus 17:7 adds another important connection: "They shall no more offer their sacrifices to demons, after whom they have played the harlot" (NKJV). Here, these demons (the ESV has "goat demons") are other gods worshiped by the cultures surrounding Israel. Again, demons are equated with pagan gods.

It is no coincidence that demonic activity is associated with religions that embrace a multitude of gods and goddesses. A desire to have supernatural contact with the spirit world often focuses people on supernatural power apart from the power God offers through a relationship with Jesus Christ and His Holy Spirit. The devil desires to be worshiped (Matthew 4:9), and demons teach false doctrine in order to deceive (1 Timothy 4:1). Those who worship false gods are, wittingly or unwittingly, pledging their allegiance to evil spirits who desire to usurp God's rightful place in their hearts.

To the Christian, an idol is "nothing" (1 Corinthians 8:4). That is, demons and their deceit have no true power over us. Any power they wield pales in comparison with the power of Christ (see Mark 5:7–8).

48. Can demons attach themselves to nonliving/inanimate objects?

There is no biblical support for the idea that demons can attach themselves to physical objects. Demon-possessed dolls, cursed necklaces, evil talismans, and satanic houses—or even cars—are the stuff of movies, books, and urban legends. The belief that a demon can possess or attach itself to an inanimate object has its roots in superstition and the occult practices of animistic cultures.

Some cite an event in the early church in Ephesus as proof that demons can fasten on to physical objects. After people in Ephesus started getting saved, "a number of them who had been practicing sorcery brought their incantation books and burned them at a public bonfire. The value of the books was several million dollars" (Acts 19:19 NLT). But the text never says that the former magicians burned their books to rid them of demons. It is more likely that these new believers destroyed their magic books to prevent the spread of lies and to show their friends and neighbors that they were now believers in Jesus.

The Bible contains accounts of demons afflicting or possessing people and animals. But there are no biblical accounts of demons being in or attached to objects. Neither does the Bible warn us about the possibility of demons attaching themselves to objects. Occult practices may attract evil spirits, and, since certain objects are used in those practices, it might seem that the demons are attracted to the objects; however, this does not mean the demons possess the objects. It is the occult activity itself—and the sinful heart of the practitioner—that attracts them. When former witches and sorcerers come to Christ, they are often advised to get rid of their occult books and objects, not because the objects have demons in them but because that paraphernalia would be a source of future temptation.

Believers in Christ are not to fear demons, although we are to be vigilant and alert for their temptations (1 Peter 5:8). The key to spiritual victory is submission to God and walking in the truth of Christ each day: "Submit yourselves, then, to God. Resist the devil, and he will flee from you" (James 4:7). Those who have put their faith in Christ have nothing to fear, as the apostle John explained: "You, dear children, are from God and have overcome [Satan and his false prophets], because the one who is in you is greater than the one who is in the world" (1 John 4:4).

SECTION 7

Questions About the Nephilim

49. Who are the sons of God and daughters of men in Genesis 6:1–4?

Genesis 6:1–4 refers to "sons of God" and "daughters of men" (NKJV). There have been several suggestions as to who the sons of God were and why their children grew into a race of giants. Here is the biblical record:

> The sons of God saw the daughters of men, that they were beautiful; and they took wives for themselves of all whom they chose. . . . There were giants [Hebrew, *nephilim*] on the earth in those days, and also afterward, when the sons of God came in to the daughters of men and they bore children to them. Those were the mighty men who were of old, men of renown.
>
> Genesis 6:2, 4 NKJV

There are three primary views concerning the identity of the sons of God:

1. They were fallen angels.
2. They were powerful human rulers.
3. They were godly descendants of Seth who intermarried with wicked descendants of Cain.

Giving weight to the first theory is the fact that in the Old Testament the phrase *sons of God* elsewhere refers to angels (Job 1:6; 2:1; 38:7). A potential problem with this is Matthew 22:30, which indicates that angels do not marry. The Bible gives no reason to believe that angels have a gender or the ability to reproduce. The other two views do not present this problem.

The weakness of views 2 and 3 is that ordinary human males marrying ordinary human females does not account for why the offspring were "giants" or "heroes of old, men of renown." Further, why would God bring the flood on the earth when God never forbade powerful human males or descendants of Seth to marry ordinary human females or descendants of Cain? The oncoming judgment of Genesis 6:5–7 is directly linked to what took place in Genesis 6:1–4. Such a harsh judgment points to a perverse sin—and the mating of fallen angels with human females would seem to qualify.

As noted, the weakness of view 1 is that Jesus declares that "at the resurrection people will neither marry nor be given in marriage; they will be like the angels in heaven" (Matthew 22:30). However, the text does not say that angels *cannot* marry, only that they *do not*. Further, marriage is not the same as sexual relations. Jesus' words do not rule out the possibility that angels could assume physical form and engage in sexual intercourse. Also, Matthew 22:30 refers to "angels in heaven," not fallen angels, who do not care about God's created order and who actively seek ways to disrupt God's plan. The fact that God's holy angels do not marry does not mean that demons cannot pervert sexuality in this world.

We believe the first view is the best interpretation. Whereas angels are spiritual beings (Hebrews 1:14), they can appear in human, physical form (Mark 16:5). The men of Sodom wanted to have sex with the two angels who were with Lot (Genesis 19:1–5). It is plausible that angels are capable of taking on human form, even to the point of replicating human sexuality. Why do the fallen angels not repeat this sin more often? It seems that God imprisoned the fallen angels who engaged in that particular evil as a warning to others not to do the same (see Jude 1:6). Early Jewish interpreters and apocryphal and pseudepigraphal writings are unanimous in holding the view that fallen angels are the sons of God mentioned in Genesis 6. This by no means closes the debate; however, the view that Genesis 6:1–4 involves fallen angels mating with human females has a strong contextual, grammatical, and historical basis.

50. Are demons the disembodied spirits of the Nephilim?

The view that the "sons of God" in Genesis 6:2 were fallen angels who mated with human women leads to the view that their offspring, the Nephilim, were a human/demonic hybrid. Accepting that theory as true, another question arises: What happened to the spirits of the Nephilim after they were killed in the flood?

Some speculate that the disembodied spirits of the Nephilim remained on the earth and became what we now refer to as demons. The presumption is that, as a hybrid, a Nephilim spirit would be different from a disembodied human spirit, which does not have the ability to remain on earth without a physical body. In Scripture, demons seem desirous of occupying a physical body of some kind (see Luke 11:24–26 and Mark 5:12). This desire would make sense if demons are Nephilim who, having lost their physical bodies in the flood, are seeking to regain that state of existence.

The idea that demons are the disembodied spirits of the Nephilim is also drawn from the Book of Enoch, which says this:

> And now, the giants, who are produced from the spirits and flesh, shall be called evil spirits upon the earth, and on the earth shall be their dwelling. Evil spirits have proceeded from their bodies; because they are born from men, and from the holy Watchers is their beginning and primal origin; they shall be evil spirits on earth, and evil spirits shall they be called. . . . And the spirits of the giants afflict, oppress, destroy, attack, do battle, and work destruction on the earth, and cause trouble.
>
> 1 Enoch 15:8–9, 11

While the Book of Enoch contains some truth (Jude 1:14), it is not the inspired, inerrant, and authoritative Word of God. We should not base a belief exclusively, or even primarily, on extra-biblical literature. So, with no need to explain the existence of demons apart from the fallen angels, and with no evidence in Scripture for the spirits of the Nephilim continuing on the earth, we have no solid reason to associate demons with the spirits of the Nephilim.

A better explanation, in our view, for what happened to the spirits of the Nephilim is that they are part of the "spirits in prison" mentioned in 1 Peter 3:19 (ESV; see also Jude 1:6). These imprisoned spirits cannot comprise *all* of the fallen angels who rebelled against God—after all, Satan, the leader of the rebellion, is not himself imprisoned. So, the "spirits in prison" should be understood to be fallen angels who participated in an *additional* rebellion, namely, the sons-of-God/daughters-of-men incident. Only those fallen angels who mated with human females—and their Nephilim offspring—are currently imprisoned.

51. Are the Anunnaki in the *Epic of Gilgamesh* the Nephilim mentioned in the Bible?

Ancient Sumer-Babylon, like many cultures of antiquity, produced mythologies to explain the world around them. The *Epic of Gilgamesh* is one such mythology. Several versions of the epic poem exist, but the twelve-tablet Akkadian version is the best known. The story centers on the friendship between the principal character, Gilgamesh, and Enkidu. Gilgamesh, the king of Uruk, is two-thirds god and one-third man. He has oppressed the people of Uruk, so the gods create Enkidu to distract Gilgamesh. Their unlikely friendship results in a journey of fantastical adventures resulting in the death of Enkidu.

An important feature of this epic is a "flood" story in which a character named Utnapishtim and his wife survive a great flood and obtain immortality. The existence of this flood story, with its many similarities to the Genesis account, indicates a common source. Rather than the Genesis flood account being copied from the *Epic of Gilgamesh*, both accounts are entirely separate records of something that actually occurred, namely, a global flood.

The gods who appear in the *Epic of Gilgamesh* are the Anunnaki, a name that probably means "those of royal blood" or "princely offspring" in the ancient Sumerian language. In contrast to this pagan mythology is the biblical account of the Nephilim. According to the Bible, the Nephilim were the descendants of the sons of God and daughters of men (Genesis 6:1–4). While there are differing interpretations of this passage, GotQuestions.org believes it involves the fallen angels (sons of God) taking on human form and mating with the daughters of men (human females), thereby producing a race of angelic-human half-breeds.

Is there a connection between the Anunnaki and the Nephilim? Perhaps. It is interesting to note that both the biblical flood account and the *Epic of Gilgamesh* mention supernatural, godlike beings interacting with humanity in connection with a global flood.

So, it is possible that the myths regarding the Anunnaki originate in the reality that was the Nephilim.

52. Was Goliath one of the Nephilim?

Who and what the Nephilim were is up for debate. Before the flood, there were Nephilim that were the offspring of "the sons of God" and "the daughters of men" (see Genesis 6:1–4 NKJV). The meaning of this passage is disputed, but it seems that angelic beings were cohabiting with human women. Regardless of their specific DNA, the Nephilim were extraordinary—they are called "the heroes of old, men of renown" (Genesis 6:4).

All the Nephilim would have been killed in the flood, as only Noah and his immediate family were spared that judgment. Nevertheless, the text indicates that the Nephilim also existed after the flood—they were "on the earth in those days—and also afterward"—that is, after the flood (Genesis 6:4). It could be that other fallen angels repeated the sin of the "sons of God," resulting in more Nephilim after the flood.

If the Nephilim were a race of gigantic warriors before the flood, it is possible that giant warriors after the flood were also called Nephilim. A modern parallel might be the "modern superhero." Everyone knows that Superman, Spider-Man, and Wonder Woman do not exist in real life, but the mythology of the superhero is firmly planted in our collective psyche. When, on occasion, a policeman, firefighter, or a member of the armed forces performs some extraordinarily heroic and dangerous rescue, the news media might refer to that person as a "real-life superhero." They do not mean that this person is actually endowed with superhuman powers, but that his behavior goes so far beyond the ordinary that he is living up to the commonly accepted mythology. This is a possibility in the Old Testament as well: any time an exceptional warrior was found, he was called a "Nephilim" without necessarily implying that he was the offspring of the "sons of God" in Genesis 6. This could explain how giants—fearfully large and ferocious warriors—are called Nephilim after the flood.

In Numbers, Moses sends twelve spies into the land of Canaan. All the spies agreed that the land was good with plenty to offer, but ten of the spies also were fearful that Israel could not take the land because of the people living in it: "The land we explored devours those living in it. All the people we saw there are of great size. We saw the Nephilim there (the descendants of Anak come from the Nephilim). We seemed like grasshoppers in our own eyes, and we looked the same to them" (Numbers 13:32–33). Here the descendants of Anak are described as coming from the Nephilim and are associated with men of great size—giants. The best explanation seems to be that the word *Nephilim* had become a semi-technical term for "giant warrior." It may have held some overtones of mystery as well, similar to the modern term *monster*, which can refer to size, as in *monster truck*. It can also have dark overtones, referring to an evil character. And finally, a monster might be some kind of abnormal or terrifying creature. With our limited knowledge of the word *Nephilim*, the best we can say is that it appears the Nephilim were gigantic, mysterious warriors of uncertain heritage. To the people who observed them, they seemed to be unnaturally formidable, large, and fierce.

Of all the giants, Goliath is the most infamous, although the Bible never associates the term *Nephilim* with him. Goliath challenged the armies of Israel, and only David was brave enough (because he trusted fully in God) to challenge him in battle. Goliath is described this way: "His height was six cubits and a span. He had a bronze helmet on his head and wore a coat of scale armor of bronze weighing five thousand shekels; on his legs he wore bronze greaves, and a bronze javelin was slung on his back. His spear shaft was like a weaver's rod, and its iron point weighed six hundred shekels" (1 Samuel 17:4–7). The footnotes in the NIV explain the ancient measurements: Goliath's height was about nine feet, nine inches. His bronze coat of armor weighed about 125 pounds, and his spearhead weighed about 15 pounds. Of course, Goliath fell at the hand of David. God is stronger than giants.

Second Samuel 21 records the demise of several giant Philistine warriors, all said to be descended from Rapha in Gath. (Since one of the men is Goliath's brother, we can assume that Goliath is descended from Rapha as well):

> Once again there was a battle between the Philistines and Israel. David went down with his men to fight against the Philistines, and he became exhausted. And Ishbi-Benob, one of the descendants of Rapha, whose bronze spearhead weighed three hundred shekels [7.5 pounds] and who was armed with a new sword, said he would kill David. But Abishai son of Zeruiah came to David's rescue; he struck the Philistine down and killed him. Then David's men swore to him, saying, "Never again will you go out with us to battle, so that the lamp of Israel will not be extinguished."
>
> 2 Samuel 21:15–17

Later, in other battles with the Philistines, three more descendants of Rapha were slain: Saph; the brother of Goliath, "who had a spear with a shaft like a weaver's rod"; and "a huge man with six fingers on each hand and six toes on each foot—twenty-four in all" (2 Samuel 21:18–22). All of these warriors were related to Goliath, but none are called Nephilim.

There are a couple of other giants mentioned in Scripture. Og, king of Bashan, was a huge man with a huge bed (Deuteronomy 3:11). One of David's mighty men, Benaiah, "struck down Moab's two mightiest warriors. He also went down into a pit on a snowy day and killed a lion. And he struck down an Egyptian who was five cubits tall. Although the Egyptian had a spear like a weaver's rod in his hand, Benaiah went against him with a club. He snatched the spear from the Egyptian's hand and killed him with his own spear" (1 Chronicles 11:22–23). Although we don't know how thick a weaver's rod was, it would have to be sufficiently strong and thick enough to support the stress of weaving, and, from the way it is used in conjunction with giant warriors, we can infer that it must have been quite large.

GuinnessWorldRecords.com reports Robert Wadlow, born in 1918, to be the tallest man in modern history. He grew to a height of just over 8 feet 11 inches.[1] However, he and many other modern "giants" suffered from health problems that would not make them good "warriors." More modest giants who are able to play professional sports are a bit smaller but still gigantic compared to the average person. There have been a good many NBA players who have been seven feet, six inches tall. There is no shortage of NFL players who stand six feet, five inches or taller and weigh in at over 350 pounds. Professional wrestling has also had a few giants, including Andre the Giant, who was seven feet, four inches tall and weighed over 500 pounds. It is quite possible that, at an earlier time, there was greater variation within the human gene pool, which could have produced even larger giants than we have among us today.

Goliath was very likely not the offspring of humans and angels, and he is never called a Nephilim; however, he was a fierce, gigantic warrior and might have been described, in the parlance of the Philistines or Israelites, as a "modern-day Nephilim."

53. Who were the Rephaim?

There are several passages in the Old Testament that speak of the Rephaim (or Rephaites), and the context describes them as giants. The name of these people literally means "terrible ones."

The Hebrew word *Rephaim* has two distinct meanings: First, in poetic literature it refers to departed spirits whose dwelling place was Sheol. It is a figurative description of the dead, similar to our concept of a ghost. The second meaning of *Rephaim* is "a mighty people with tall stature who lived in Canaan." The word doesn't seem to be ethnocentric like "Jew" or "Egyptian" but is more of a descriptive term. This second meaning will be the focus of this answer.

The first reference to the Rephaim is Genesis 14:5, when the Rephaim, Zuzim, and Emim people were defeated in a battle with Kedorlaomer and his allies. When the Israelites first approached the Promised Land after the Exodus from Egypt, they were afraid to enter the land because it was filled with "giants" (the word used in Numbers 13:33 is *Nephilim*), the sons of Anak. Giants were widely scattered through Canaan, but were known by different local names, including Rephaim, Zuzim, Emim, and Anakim. Deuteronomy 2:20–21 says the Rephaim were strong and tall, like the Anakites. Og, king of Bashan, was described as the last of the Rephaim in his land (Deuteronomy 3:11), and his bed was thirteen feet long and six feet wide.

Is it possible that the Rephaim were literal giants? The Septuagint uses the Greek words *gigas* and *titanes* (the source of the English *titan*) to translate these and other verses, so the ancient Jews certainly considered them to be giants. They are described generally as being between seven and ten feet tall and are called "mighty men." The Egyptians wrote about giants who lived in the land of Canaan, and the folklore of other nations is full of such references. The people of the ancient world accepted the presence of giants as a fact of history, and the Bible presents them as enemies who were destroyed either by the direct judgment of God or indirectly through battle with men.

So where did these giants come from? One theory, based on Genesis 6:1–4, is that fallen angels (the sons of God) had sexual relations with women, resulting in the birth of giants. This is remarkably similar to Greek and Roman myths about demigods, but the theory has some theological and biological obstacles. Another theory, also based on Genesis 6, is that the fallen angels, having knowledge of human genetics, indwelt certain men and women who would have the right traits to produce a race of giants and induced them to cohabit with each other. A third theory is that the giants were simply the result of normal genetic variability within a society. Whatever the origin of the Rephaim, it is certain that a race of "giants"—strong, tall people—did exist at one time, and many cultures had dealings with them. Even today, there are people who grow to extreme sizes, whether through genetic disorders like gigantism or through normal heredity.

54. Are there descendants of the Nephilim in the world today?

There is much mystery surrounding the Nephilim. Most of the information about them comes from Genesis 6:4: "The Nephilim were on the earth in those days—and also afterward—when the sons of God went to the daughters of humans and had children by them. They were the heroes of old, men of renown." Almost everything about this verse is difficult to understand. Is *Nephilim* a specific technical term, or is it descriptive, based on what the word itself means? And what the word means is uncertain. It seems to have something to do with falling—Nephilim are possibly "fallen ones" or "ones who cause others to fall." Also, who are the "sons of God"? Are they human or some kind of angelic beings? If the sons of God are angelic, then is the angelic/human crossbreeding what accounts for the greatness of the Nephilim?

However these questions are answered, we would assume that all the Nephilim alive at the time of Noah perished in the flood. Interestingly, though, Genesis 6:4 indicates that the Nephilim reappeared after the flood: They were "on the earth in those days—and also afterward"—that is, after the flood.

In Moses' day, the spies brought back their reports about the Promised Land. All the spies agreed that the land was good with bounty to offer; however, ten of the spies were fearful that Israel could not take the land because of the people living in it: "The land we explored devours those living in it. All the people we saw there are of great size. We saw the Nephilim there (the descendants of Anak come from the Nephilim). We seemed like grasshoppers in our own eyes, and we looked the same to them" (Numbers 13:32–33). Here the descendants of Anak are described as coming from the Nephilim and are associated with men of great size. This is similar to Genesis 6:4 where they are associated with "heroes of old, men of renown." In each case, Nephilim would be formidable opponents, especially in the kind of hand-to-hand combat that taking the Promised Land would require.

The Septuagint (a Greek translation of the Old Testament) translated *Nephilim* with the Greek word for "giants." This is not a direct translation of the word but an attempt to communicate the idea of what the Nephilim were. Giants are mentioned in the Old Testament several times, especially in conjunction with the Philistines—Goliath being the most prominent. These were not human-angel hybrids but very large men (see Deuteronomy 3:11).

It is quite possible that *Nephilim* simply became a semi-technical term for "giant warrior." It may have carried some nebulous idea of mystery as well. It might be similar to the modern term *monster*. That word can be used to refer to size, as in *monster truck* or *monster candy bar*. It can also have dark overtones. Describing someone as a monster can reference an evil character. And finally, a monster might be some kind of supernatural creature or even something of a hybrid like a vampire or a werewolf. With our limited knowledge of the word *Nephilim*, it appears the Nephilim were gigantic, mysterious warriors of uncertain heredity. People who observed the Nephilim considered them to be unnatural. Even today we have "giants" among us—the average NBA or NFL player is freakishly gigantic compared with most of us. This does not mean there is a race of human-angel hybrids in our midst.

It seems that the Nephilim, at least in the time of Moses and Joshua, continued in the line of the descendants of Anak, who were extremely large and fearsome. It is possible that there are descendants of those "Nephilim" today, just as today there could be distant descendants of Moabites, Amalekites, Hittites, and Babylonians.

55. Who were the spirits in prison?

The "spirits in prison" are mentioned in the broader context of suffering righteously. First Peter 3:18–20 says, "For Christ also died for sins once for all, the just for the unjust, so that He might bring us to God, having been put to death in the flesh, but made alive in the spirit; in which also He went and made proclamation to the spirits now in prison, who once were disobedient, when the patience of God kept waiting in the days of Noah, during the construction of the ark" (NASB1995). Some people use this passage to infer what Jesus did during the time that His body was in the grave.

We know three things for sure about the spirits mentioned in 1 Peter 3:19. They are incorporeal, they are imprisoned, and their sin was committed before the flood. Their relation to Jesus and the nature of His announcement to them are open to speculation. Who exactly these spirits are has been the subject of some debate through the years. Here are two theories:

1. *The spirits in prison are fallen angels or demons.* The spirits in prison cannot be *holy* angels because the holy angels have not sinned and are not imprisoned. And not all the fallen angels are imprisoned, of course, for the New Testament gives many examples of demonic activity on earth. That leaves a select group of demons who, unlike their fellow demons, are held captive.

What might be a reason for some, but not all, of the demons to be imprisoned? Jude 1:6 gives us an important clue: "The angels who did not keep their positions of authority but abandoned their proper dwelling—these he has kept in darkness, bound with everlasting chains for judgment on the great Day." Some of the fallen angels committed an egregious crime of some kind; Jude 1:6 does not give details, but the demons' sin was related to how they "did not keep their own position but deserted their proper dwelling" (HCSB). Revelation 9:1–12, 14–15, and 2 Peter 2:4 also speak of a group of wicked angels that are currently bound.

If the spirits in prison are fallen angels, the sin they committed could be the one in Genesis 6:1–4, which records the "sons of God" mating with the "daughters of men" and producing a race of giants, the Nephilim. If the "sons of God" were fallen angels, then the sin of Genesis 6 involved angels leaving the place where they belonged in an act of disobedience before the flood—and that corresponds to what the apostle mentions in 1 Peter 3:19. It could be that the demons who cohabited with human women were imprisoned by God to prevent them from repeating that sin and to discourage other demons from trying it.

According to 1 Peter 3:19, Jesus "made proclamation" to these spirits in prison. The Greek word translated "proclaimed" or "preached" means "to publicly declare" or "to herald." If the spirits are demons, then Peter says that Jesus went to the Abyss and proclaimed His victory to the fallen angels imprisoned there. They had lost, and He had won. The cross triumphs over all evil (see Colossians 2:15).

2. *The spirits in prison are the human spirits of those who perished in the flood of Noah's day.* As for Christ preaching to them, there are three possible interpretations: (a) Christ preached to them figuratively, in and through Noah, while they were in the flesh; (b) Christ preached to them literally, being present with Noah through the Holy Spirit who inspired Noah to proclaim the message of coming judgment; and (c) Christ preached to them literally in between His death and resurrection. According to each of these interpretations, the spirits are called such because they existed in a spiritual condition when Peter wrote; they were no longer in the flesh but lived in Hades/hell.

SECTION 8

Questions About Types of Demons

56. Are there different types of demons?

The Bible does not say much about different types of demons. But, over the years, various writers of theological works have speculated on different classifications for demons. One of the oldest is the pseudepigraphical Testament of Solomon. During the Middle Ages, demons were often classified based on the sins they promoted or other activities they engaged in. For instance, each of the "seven deadly sins" was said to have a specific demon behind it.

The Bible is our only reliable source of information about demons, and the information it contains about them is sparse. The Bible says nothing directly about classifications or kinds of demons. Jesus mentions a unique "kind" of evil spirit in Mark 9:29, but He does not name it. Much of the information we have about demons is simply inferred from biblical passages in which they play a role. Christian ministries that focus on deliverance from demons place more emphasis on them than the Bible does.

A detailed but highly speculative demonology has sprung up in some religious and charismatic circles. Various evil spirits are dubbed as "Jezebels," "pythons," "Delilahs," "mermaids," "Absaloms," etc. None of this is biblical. Scripture gives no reason to believe there are specific classes of demons or that Christians today have the gift of rebuking or exorcising them.

Perhaps the most extensive passage on spiritual warfare in the New Testament, Ephesians 6:10–18 (concerning the full armor of God), mentions that "our struggle is not against flesh and blood, but against the rulers, against the authorities, against the powers of this dark world and against the spiritual forces of evil in the heavenly realms" (Ephesians 6:12). However, the emphasis here is on the weapons God provides for victory; there is no mention of techniques to bind or cast out the evil forces. Some see the "rulers," "authorities," "powers," etc., as different classifications of demons, but this is reading into the text more than it is telling us.

From the biblical evidence, we infer that demons are fallen angels that followed Satan when he rebelled. Revelation 12 says that a dragon (Satan) swept one third of the stars from heaven. However, the origin of demons is far from clear, and the conclusion that they are fallen angels is disputed by some. In Revelation 12:9, we read, "The great dragon was hurled down—that ancient serpent called the devil, or Satan, who leads the whole world astray. He was hurled to the earth, and his angels with him." Likewise, in Matthew 25:41, Jesus says that on Judgment Day He will say to some people, "Depart from me, you who are cursed, into the eternal fire prepared for the devil and his angels." This may mean that the demons are fallen angels who fell when Satan did, or it might mean that demons are called "angels" in the basic sense that they are Satan's "messengers" (the literal meaning of the word *angels*).

With certainty we can say that demons are the messengers or minions of Satan. The word *demon* is not used in the Old Testament (although evil spirits are mentioned), but by the time of the New Testament, Jewish theologians had done a lot of speculating about them. The concept of demons or evil spirits was also common in other religious thought at the time. The Gospels seem to assume that much of what was thought about demons at the time is true. We see Jesus casting out demons (e.g., Matthew 8:28–33), and we see that they are often responsible for causing physical illness, which Jesus healed by casting out the demon (e.g., Matthew 9:33). Paul tells us that demons are behind the worship of pagan gods and that a sacrifice to an idol is really a sacrifice to a demon (1 Corinthians 10:19–20).

Whenever there are gaps in our knowledge, it is natural to want to fill them in. However, in the case of demonology, most of the "filler" information is unfounded and sometimes lurid speculation. We know that demons are evil spirits who, in concert with and following the directives of Satan, war against God and mankind. It is probably accurate to think of them as counterparts to the holy angels that minister to people on God's behalf. We know that they have been defeated in principle by Christ on the cross and that their final destination will be eternal torment in a place prepared for them (Matthew 25:41).

57. What does it mean that the name of the demon was Legion?

In Mark 5, Jesus visits the region of the Gerasenes and is immediately confronted by a demon-possessed man who lived among the tombs, cut himself with stones, and could not be kept in captivity (Mark 5:1–5). When Jesus asked the demon what its name was, the demon replied, "My name is Legion . . . for we are many" (Mark 5:9).

In common usage, a legion was the largest unit in the Roman army. At that time, a legion averaged about five thousand fighting men, though it could have thousands more or fewer. So, the term *legion* refers to any large number—a multitude. When the demon in Mark 5 said that its name was Legion, it meant that the demoniac of the Gerasenes was possessed by a large number of unclean spirits.

Scripture does not say exactly how many demons comprised the Legion within the man. However, when Jesus cast them out, they entered a herd of pigs feeding nearby. Legion caused the pigs to rush down a hillside and into the sea, where they were all drowned (Mark 5:13). The number of pigs killed was "about two thousand." That detail suggests that Legion was composed of about two thousand demons. The large number of demons may account for the afflicted man's untamable nature and great strength—strength that was no match for God, of course.

There is one other mention of a "legion" in the context of spirit beings, this time of good angels. When Jesus was being arrested, Peter pulled out a sword and wounded a nearby member of the mob. Jesus healed the wound (Luke 22:51) and told Peter to put away his sword (Matthew 26:52). The Lord reminded Peter that, if He needed help, He could have God send "more than twelve legions of angels" (Matthew 26:53). That might total sixty thousand angels, but the exact number wasn't the point. Jesus was reminding the terrified disciples that God is always in control of all circumstances, even during the horrible injustice of the murder of His own Son.

It is interesting that the Bible refers to both holy angels and demons as forming legions. *Legion* is a military term, one that fits the Bible's descriptions of spiritual warfare in several places (Daniel 10:13; Ephesians 6:12; Revelation 12:7).

How can we stand against such numerous and powerful foes? God completely equips believers for battle against satanic forces: "Put on the full armor of God, so that when the day of evil comes, you may be able to stand your ground" (Ephesians 6:13). As Christians, we are "more than conquerors" through Christ (Romans 8:37). Jesus is our Commander. He is the One who dispatched the demons named Legion with just a word. And He will one day throw Legion and all the other demons "into the eternal fire prepared for the devil and his angels" (Matthew 25:41; cf. Revelation 20:10).

58. What are familiar spirits?

The word *familiar* is from the Latin *familiaris*, meaning a "household servant" or "one who is closely acquainted." In centuries past, the term *familiar spirit* or *familiar* expressed the idea that sorcerers and witches had spirits to guide them or act as their servants. A familiar spirit was often thought to take the form of an animal such as a dog, a butterfly, a rabbit—or the proverbial black cat. Spiritists, even to this day, usually have a "spirit guide" who communicates with them, and it is becoming popular even in general conversation to speak of a person's "spirit animal." These are familiar spirits.

Leviticus 19:31 refers to "mediums and familiar spirits" (NKJV). The warning in the NIV is "Do not turn to mediums or seek out spiritists [familiar spirits], for you will be defiled by them. I am the LORD your God" (cf. Deuteronomy 18:9–14). A medium is one who acts as a liaison to supposedly communicate with the dead on behalf of the living. In reality, mediums are contacting demons who convince the mediums that they are "familiar" and can be trusted and believed. The practice of witchcraft, sorcery, and anything associated with familiar spirits was banned in Israel (see Leviticus 20:6, 27).

Familiar spirits and spirit guides are under the control of their master, Satan. They influence people to spread lies and deceit in order to thwart the kingdom of God. To knowingly open oneself to the work of demons is an evil thing: "Let no one be found among you who sacrifices his son or daughter in fire, who practices divination or sorcery, interprets omens, engages in witchcraft, or casts spells, or who is a medium or spiritist or who consults the dead. Anyone who does these things is detestable to the Lord" (Deuteronomy 18:10–12).

Some avenues through which demons or "familiar spirits" can gain entrance into a person's life are divination, transcendental meditation, New Age visualization, necromancy, witchcraft, and drug and alcohol abuse. These are all activities that believers are exhorted to avoid. We are to be filled with the Holy Spirit, with love, with joy, and with the fullness of life that comes from Jesus Christ. We are to listen to God alone and be on guard, "for our struggle is not against flesh and blood, but against the rulers, against the authorities, against the powers of this dark world and against the spiritual forces of evil in the heavenly realms" (Ephesians 6:12).

59. What does the Bible say about hereditary spirits?

Some "deliverance ministries" and charismatic groups teach the existence of hereditary spirits, also called generational spirits or familial spirits. These entities are thought to be evil spirits that attach themselves to a particular family and harass them through multiple generations. They are demons inherited from one's ancestors.

Those who teach the existence of hereditary spirits consider them the source of various sins such as pride, lust, perversion, anger, rebellion, fear, and addiction. Generational or hereditary spirits are blamed for "generational curses" that result in poverty, sickness, disease, confusion, failure, and even death. According to the concept of generational spirits, a man struggles with anger issues because he's being influenced by an "anger demon"—the same demon who provoked his father and grandfather to anger. A woman who struggles with depression is being oppressed by a "depression demon" that was invited into the family by the sin of an ancestor—one who practiced witchcraft, perhaps. Once attached to the family, the demon causes trouble down the lineage.

Usually, deliverance ministries recommend that a person renounce the generational spirits and all the curses his or her family is under, "binding" and "rebuking" all the demons, ordering sickness away, etc. (This must be done out loud, so the demons can hear the rebuke.) The idea is that one must cast out all the demons and break all pacts with the devil made by ancestors. Only then is one free to grow spiritually in Christ.

The idea of hereditary spirits or generational spirits has more in common with paganism than it does with the Bible. Neopagans and Wiccans readily admit a belief in generational curses, demons that attach themselves to a certain family, and the idea that occult power can be passed down through one's family line. In paganism, breaking a generational curse often involves working with one's (dead) ancestors.

The teaching of generational spirits has no biblical foundation. Some try to defend a belief in generational spirits by pointing to passages such as Deuteronomy 5:9, "I, the LORD your God, am a jealous God, punishing the children for the sin of the parents to the third and fourth generation of those who hate me." However, it's important to note that this passage (and others such as Exodus 20:5 and Numbers 14:18) does not mention any *spirits*. We might call God's punishment here a "generational curse," but the text references no generational or hereditary spirit. God was disciplining the rebellious in Israel, but demons are not said to be involved.

The effects of sin (specifically idolatry in Deuteronomy 5) are naturally passed down from one generation to the next. God's punishment of someone's children, grandchildren, and great-grandchildren has nothing to do with familial demons and everything to do with the consequence of bad choices that affect others in the family. Any type of sinful choice can possibly impact several generations of one's offspring and cause much suffering.

Further, when a father has a sinful lifestyle, his children are likely to practice the same sinful lifestyle. Implied in the warning of Exodus 20:5 is the fact that children will choose to repeat the sins of their fathers. God promises to punish sin to the third or fourth generation because those generations are committing the same sins their fathers did. But nothing in the Mosaic Law suggests a demon attaching itself to a family.

Also of note, God's warning to visit iniquity on future generations is part of the Old Testament Law, not New Testament grace. A generational curse was a consequence experienced by a specific nation (Israel) for a specific sin (idolatry). The history books of the Old Testament (especially Judges) contain the record of this divine punishment meted out.

The idea that every sin or problem today can be blamed on a generational curse is unbiblical. The idea of a generational spirit is even less biblical. It is unfortunate that some today are deceived by various notions borrowed from pagan practices, bundled with biblical truth and presented as proper for Christians.

For someone worried about a generational curse or a hereditary spirit, the answer is salvation in Jesus Christ. A Christian is a new creation (2 Corinthians 5:17). How can a child of God be under God's curse (Romans 8:1)? Why should one redeemed by God and indwelt by the Holy Spirit fear any demon? "You, dear children, are from God and have overcome them, because the one who is in you is greater than the one who is in the world" (1 John 4:4).

Yes, God promised to visit Israel's sin upon the third and fourth generations, but we need to keep reading. In the very next verse, He promised that He would show "love to a thousand generations of those who love me and keep my commandments" (Exodus 20:6). In other words, God's grace lasts a thousand times longer than His wrath.

60. What are territorial spirits?

Territorial spirits is a term some Christians use to identify demonic occupation of a specific geographic location. Ironically, it is also a term pagans use to describe an otherworldly presence believed to be residing in a specific geographical location.

The Christian concept of territorial spirits comes from passages such as Daniel 10; John 12:31; John 14:30; John 16:11; Mark 5:10; and Ephesians 6:12. All of these passages imply that fallen angels have been given some type of responsibility over a certain area, though the Bible never explicitly delineates a hierarchy of demonic activity in specific regions of the world. Whether or not demons are assigned a specific region, the Bible is clear that demons are at work in the world and that believers are very much involved in a spiritual battle against them.

In Daniel 10, for example, an angel struggled against a demonic adversary the entire time Daniel was praying and fasting. It wasn't until the end of Daniel's spiritually focused time that the angel finally broke away and came to Daniel. Ephesians 6 exhorts believers to stand firm against our spiritual adversaries and to remain alert and ready for battle. There is no doubt that our struggle on Earth is mirrored in some way in the spiritual realm.

The problem inherent in the term *territorial spirits* is that some Christians believe it is their duty to engage territorial demons in spiritual warfare. This, however, cannot be justified by Scripture. There is not a single instance in the Bible where someone actively sought out a demon in order to engage it. Demon-possessed individuals were encountered, and some were brought to Jesus and His disciples for healing, but the disciples didn't go looking for demons to cast out of people. No one in the Bible ever prayed that the "demon princes" of a town be "bound" from working their will against the residents of that town.

Territorial spirits, although not explicitly a scriptural idea, may very well exist, as seen in the previous passages. More important than whether a spirit is "territorial" is our response. A believer in Christ has no biblical support to seek out and confront demons. Rather, a believer needs to be aware of spiritual battles and take them seriously (1 Peter 5:8). Our lives need to be focused on prayer and on growing in faith. Should we ever encounter a demon, we definitely have the Christ-given authority to deal with it, but we should not go looking for them, territorial or otherwise.

61. What does the Bible say about transferring spirits?

The idea behind "transferring spirits" is that someone can transfer an evil spirit to another person by touching or being near him. Those who teach this concept tell others not to associate with friends or family members who might transfer such a spirit into them. There is no scriptural basis for the concept of transferring spirits by touching or being near another person or by any other method. Of course, we can be affected by negative attitudes or sinful behaviors in others, but to identify these as spirit beings that can be transferred to others is unbiblical.

The Bible says there are two types of created spirit beings, the unfallen, holy angels and the angels who followed Satan in his rebellion. Angels who have not sinned are called ministering spirits (Hebrews 1:14), and we are told that God sends them forth to minister to those who will be heirs of salvation, that is, those who believe in Christ as Savior. Angels who joined Satan in his rebellion constitute the horde of spiritual beings (demons) dedicated to evil.

The Bible records only one instance of demons being transferred from one living creature to another. It happened when Jesus transferred the legion of demons from the possessed men into the herd of pigs (Matthew 8:28–34). Jesus did not repeat this miracle, nor did He ever warn His disciples (or us) about transferring spirits. There is no reason for a born-again believer in Christ to fear Satan or his fallen angels. If we resist him, he will flee from us. "Submit yourselves therefore to God. Resist the devil, and he will flee from you" (James 4:7 KJV). As believers, our body is the temple of the Holy Spirit. We can be confident that the Holy Spirit will not tolerate a demon in His temple.

62. Is there an angel of death?

The idea of an "angel of death" is present in several religions. The "angel of death" is known as Samael, Sariel, or Azrael in Judaism; as Malak Almawt in Islam; as Yama or Yamaraj in Hinduism; and as the Grim Reaper in popular fiction. In various mythologies, the angel of death is imagined as anything from a cloaked skeletal figure with a sickle, to a beautiful woman, to a small child. While the details vary, the core belief is that a being comes to a person at the moment of death, either actually causing death or simply observing it—with the purpose of then taking the person's soul to the abode of the dead.

This "angel of death" concept is not taught in the Bible. The Bible nowhere teaches that there is a particular angel who is in charge of death or who is present whenever a person dies. Second Kings 19:35 describes an angel putting to death 185,000 Assyrians who had invaded Israel. Some also see Exodus chapter 12, the death of the firstborn of Egypt, as the work of an angel. While this is possible, the Bible nowhere attributes the death of the firstborn to an angel. Whatever the case, while the Bible describes angels causing death at the command of the Lord, Scripture nowhere teaches that there is a specific angel of death.

God, and God alone, is sovereign over the timing of our deaths. No angel or demon can cause our death before the time God has willed it to occur. According to Romans 6:23 and Revelation 20:11–15, death is separation—separation of our soul-spirit from our body (physical death) and, in the case of unbelievers, everlasting separation from God (eternal death). Death is something that occurs. Death is not an angel, a demon, a person, or any other being. Angels may be able to cause death and may be involved in what happens to us after death—but there is no such thing as an "angel of death."

63. What is a spirit of infirmity?

The term *spirit of infirmity* occurs in Luke 13:11 specifically in the KJV. Here a woman who had been crippled for eighteen years is healed by Jesus on the Sabbath day. Luke says she had a "spirit of infirmity" or a "disabling spirit" (ESV) or a "sickness caused by a spirit" (NASB) or was "crippled by a spirit" (NIV). Quite simply, this "spirit of infirmity" is a demon who caused the woman to be crippled for eighteen years.

The Bible teaches the fact of spiritual warfare. Ephesians 6:12 says, "For our struggle is not against flesh and blood, but against the rulers, against the authorities, against the powers of this dark world and against the spiritual forces of evil in the heavenly realms." And from Luke 13 we know that evil spirits can sometimes cause physical maladies. However, it is not clear that there are specific spirits whose "specialty" is such things as sickness or poverty or anger. Luke's reference to the "spirit of infirmity" indicates that, at least in that one case, a demon had been granted power to inflict a disability. Extrapolating a doctrine that categorizes demons according to the afflictions they cause goes beyond what the Bible teaches.

We need to be careful not to overemphasize the power of demons. Many human ailments are simply caused by living in a fallen world, and there are many instances in Luke's Gospel of people being healed of diseases with no mention of a demonic cause. In Luke 13 Jesus specifically speaks of Satan having bound this woman (v. 16). But, in many other cases of healing, He simply heals with no mention of evil spirits involved.

Today, there are some people who refer to "spirits of infirmity" as being the cause for sickness. Or they may talk about "spirits of" particular emotions or sins, such as anger or lust. Certainly, Satan and his demons can attack our bodies, emotions, and thinking patterns. But we cannot blame every illness, difficult emotion, or sin on Satan's influence. There are a variety of reasons a person may be struggling with such things.

No matter the specific cause of an infirmity, we can bring the problem to God in prayer. James 4:7–8 talks about resisting the devil and submitting to God. Prayer is one way to do this. James 5:16 says we should confess our sins to one another so that we can pray for healing.

The major thing to observe from Luke 13:10–17 is the power and compassion of Jesus. In an instant, He overcame the disability this woman had been struggling with for eighteen years. He healed her on the Sabbath day, to the indignation of the Pharisees. He responded to her need with compassion, calling the woman a "daughter of Abraham" (Luke 13:16) and highlighting how much God loved her and was willing to free her.

64. What is a succubus?

According to medieval folklore, a succubus is a demon that takes the form of a woman in order to have intercourse with a man in his dreams. The word *succubus* comes from Old Latin and means "to lie under." In Islamic superstition, there is a similar demon called the *qarinah* or *karina*, and in ancient Middle Eastern cultures Lilith was the night demon's name. Whichever name is used, the essential qualities are the same: The succubus is a demon who tempts men sexually at night and who tries to kill infants at birth.

There are two ancient passages that may refer directly to this kind of demon. One of the Dead Sea Scrolls (4Q184) contains a poem commonly called "The Seductress." This poem depicts a being with "a multitude of sins" in "her skirts" who lives "in the midst of the night."[1] This evil being tempts men into sin and ultimately drags them into the Pit. The passage is similar to Proverbs 2:18–19, which describes the dangers of the seductress or "strange woman" (v. 16 KJV). In describing the results of God's judgment on Edom, Isaiah 34:14 says, "The night creature shall rest there, and find for herself a place of rest" (NKJV). The Hebrew word translated "night creature" is *liyliyth*, which can also be translated as "night monster" (NASB1995) and "Lilith (night demon)" (AMP).

Are succubi real? If we grant credence to the widespread beliefs of ancient cultures, the answer would be yes. If we limit ourselves to the biblical text, the answer becomes more difficult. The Bible certainly teaches that demons are real and that they interact with mankind. Second Peter 2:4 speaks of angels who sinned and were cast down to hell in judgment. Jude 1:6 likewise speaks of angels who "did not keep their proper domain" (NKJV) and are awaiting the final judgment. Jesus confronted demonic possession and cast demons out of people, as did His disciples. Could demonic oppression include unwanted sexual acts? Possibly.

The male counterpart of the succubus is the incubus, from the Latin *incubo* for "nightmare." An incubus supposedly lies with human women in their sleep in order to have sexual intercourse with them. In folklore, incubi were thought to be capable of fathering children, and the half-human offspring of an incubus was called a cambion. Merlin, the legendary wizard from the King Arthur tales, was supposedly sired by an incubus, from whom he received his supernatural abilities. Belief in succubi and incubi is rooted in medieval superstition most likely developed to explain natural phenomena that occur during sleep—nightmares, sexual dreams, sleep paralysis, and night terrors. The incubus was also blamed for nighttime rapes and other assaults perpetrated by very human offenders.

Some people study demons as an aid in spiritual warfare. While it is good to be vigilant and informed, our main focus should be on learning more about the One who "has delivered us from the power of darkness and conveyed us into the kingdom of the Son of His love, in whom we have redemption through His blood, the forgiveness of sins" (Colossians 1:13–14 NKJV). We need not fear succubi or incubi. We have been given the full armor of God "so that [we] will be able to stand firm against all strategies of the devil" (Ephesians 6:11 NLT).

SECTION 9
Questions About Satan

65. Who is Satan in the Bible?

The name *Satan* means "adversary." Satan is described in the Bible as an angelic enemy of God and, by extension, the enemy and opponent of those who follow God. Although everything God created was initially good (Genesis 1:31), Satan chose to rebel against the Lord, and many other angels followed his rebellion (Ezekiel 28:15; Isaiah 14:12–17). Satan tempted Eve to sin in the Garden of Eden, and Adam followed her into sin, plunging the whole human race into a curse (Genesis 3:16–19; Romans 5:12). Pictured as a serpent and dragon in the Bible (Genesis 3:1; Revelation 12:9), Satan is a murderer and the father of lies. He promotes false doctrines and craftily seeks to keep unbelievers in spiritual bondage (John 8:44; 2 Corinthians 4:4; 11:14; 1 Timothy 4:1).

There are many things said in the Bible about Satan, but it is important to also know what is not said about him. Some of the misconceptions regarding the devil include the following:

- Satan is not a personal being but only a force of evil.
- He is equal to God, with the two opposing forces creating a form of dualism.
- He resides in and is the ruler of hell.
- He can do whatever he pleases.
- He is omnipresent.
- He received a ransom payment from Jesus when Jesus died on the cross.

False ideas about Satan come from a variety of sources. For instance, the belief that the devil is equal to God and is His opposite comes from Zoroastrianism. The belief that Jesus died to pay a ransom to the devil was theorized by Origen. John Milton's *Paradise Lost*, not the Bible, describes Satan as the king of hell.[1]

Concerning Satan, the Bible gives the following information:

- Satan is a personal being, with a mind, emotions, and a will (Job 1; Matthew 4:1–12).
- He is a created being and is not equal to God (Ezekiel 28:15).
- Satan does not rule hell. Hell was created as a punishment for Satan and his demons (Matthew 25:41). Neither does Satan live in hell. The Bible describes him appearing in heaven and roaming the earth (Job 1:6–7).
- The devil can only do what God allows (Job 1:12).
- Satan is not omnipresent. But he does oversee a horde of demons, called "the powers of this dark world and . . . the spiritual forces of evil in the heavenly realms" (Ephesians 6:12). He uses this network to tempt and deceive people.

- He actively works to nullify the effect of the Word of God in people's hearts (Matthew 13:3–4, 19), and he blinds the intellect of those who do not believe so they cannot understand the gospel (2 Corinthians 4:4).

The Bible describes how Christians should be mindful of the schemes of Satan: "Be alert and of sober mind. Your enemy the devil prowls around like a roaring lion looking for someone to devour" (1 Peter 5:8). We must resist him soberly, vigilantly, and steadfastly, aware of the reality of his plans to tempt us to make us unfruitful for the Lord (2 Corinthians 2:11). When tempted, the believer should submit himself to the Lord and resist the devil, and Satan will flee (James 4:7).

In addition to being a tempter, Satan is also "the accuser of our brothers" (Revelation 12:10 ESV). He enjoys listing the many sins of believers, but the Lord Jesus, our Advocate, defeats the accusations because He has paid the price for our sins (1 John 2:1–2). Christians can be confident of their salvation because Jesus has done the work for us through His death and resurrection (Ephesians 2:8–9).

Satan is described as the "god of this age" (2 Corinthians 4:4) and has dominion over the world and its system (John 12:31; 1 John 5:19). During the tribulation, the devil will deceive the masses and raise up the Antichrist as world ruler (Revelation 13:5–8). Satan has always wanted people to worship him as God, and part of his end-times deception will be to delude the whole world (Revelation 13:3–4). Through the Antichrist, Satan will also attempt to destroy the remnant of Israel but will not be successful (Revelation 12:13–16). At the end of the tribulation, Jesus will return, the Antichrist and false prophet will be thrown into the lake of fire, and Satan will be imprisoned for a thousand years (Revelation 19:19–20; 20:1–3). After that time, Satan will be released and lead one last rebellion (Revelation 20:7–9); then Satan will finally be thrown into the lake of fire, forever to be tormented for his rebellion and works of evil (Revelation 20:10).

The dominion of Satan over the world may seem unassailable, but the devil cannot withstand the power of our Savior and Lord, Jesus Christ. In the words of Martin Luther, "His doom is sure; one little word shall fell him."[2]

66. Did God create Satan?

God created everything (John 1:3). This includes physical beings and matter as well as spiritual beings (Colossians 1:15–17). The only person who has the power of being in and of Himself—the only One with no beginning or ending—is God. He is self-existent (Exodus 3:14). All other beings were created by God and belong to God (Psalm 24:1), and this includes the being we call Satan.

When we say that God created Satan, we do not mean that God created sin. All that God made, including the angelic being who later became known as Satan, was "very good" (Genesis 1:31). God is not the author of sin, and He did not make Satan sinful. God is holy and does not create anything that is contrary to His own nature (Psalm 86:8–10; 99:1–3; Isaiah 40:25; 57:15).

The Bible's references to the king of Babylon and the king of Tyre in Isaiah 14:12–15 and Ezekiel 28:13–17, respectively, are considered by most scholars as types or figures of Satan. These two passages give us a bit of history concerning Satan and his origins. Isaiah 14:12 says Satan's beginnings were in heaven. The Ezekiel 28 passage says Satan was created (v. 13) and that he was one of the cherubim (v. 14). He was "blameless" until sin was found in him (Ezekiel 28:15).

The Bible describes the root of Satan's sin as pride (Ezekiel 28:17). Before Satan was expelled from heaven, he must have been very beautiful (Ezekiel 28:12). Scripture does not say exactly how Satan came to be sinful, but it does say that he was not always sinful: "You were blameless in all you did from the day you were created until the day evil was found in you" (Ezekiel

28:15 NLT). Satan's sin was of his own doing, and he was judged (Ezekiel 28:16–18).

So, while it is correct to say God created Satan, it's incorrect to say that God created the sin within Satan. Satan chose his own course (Isaiah 14:13). God never causes sin (James 1:13), even though He has created a world where sin is possible. Someday God is going to put an end to Satan and all sin (Revelation 20:10). The fallen angels, including Satan, will be confined to everlasting punishment.

67. How did Satan and other angels sin if heaven is sinless?

The Bible teaches that Satan was created in perfection and given a prominent position in heaven (Ezekiel 28:11–15). He was "full of wisdom and perfect in beauty" (v. 12). God appointed him the highest-ranking angel. From his place of great privilege, Satan led possibly one third of heaven's angels in a rebellion against God (Ezekiel 28:16–17; Revelation 12:4). God expelled him from heaven, casting him down to the earth (Ezekiel 28:16–18).

The sin that caused Satan to fall from heaven was pride (1 Timothy 3:6). Isaiah describes how it happened:

> How you are fallen from heaven,
>   O shining star, son of the morning!
> You have been thrown down to the earth,
>   you who destroyed the nations of the world.
> For you said to yourself,
>   "I will ascend to heaven and set my throne above God's stars.
> I will preside on the mountain of the gods far away in the north.
> I will climb to the highest heavens and be like the Most High."
> Instead, you will be brought down to the place of the dead,
>   down to its lowest depths.
>
> Isaiah 14:12–15 NLT

Demonstrating the epitome of arrogance and self-importance, Satan wanted to be like God. He used his high position for personal gain and self-promotion (Ezekiel 28:16). Rather than submit to God, Satan rebelled. He refused to worship and obey his Creator. He desired to be his own god. His sin was particularly offensive because it was a monumental abuse of privilege and power. It also had a sweeping effect on other angels (Revelation 12:7), on people (Ephesians 2:2), and on all nations of the world (Revelation 20:3).

Satan's "I will" statements present a clue as to how he and other angels could sin in heaven, even though heaven is a sinless place. God had given Satan a choice, a free will, and he exerted it. He said, "I will ascend. . . . I will preside. . . . I will climb." God gave both angels and humans free will. They were presented with a choice: to obey God or not. Satan was created in perfection, and Adam and Eve were created in God's image (Genesis 1:27; 5:1–3; 9:6; James 3:9) and placed in a perfect paradise (Genesis 2:5–25). Humans, like the angels, were given a choice to obey God (Genesis 2:15–16), but they exerted their will to disobey (Genesis 3:1–24). Their sin produced the fall of humankind, and Adam and Eve were expelled from paradise. Satan and other angels exerted their free will, and those who rebelled were expelled from heaven. God did not predispose the angels to rebel or coerce them to obey. The angels who sinned did so knowingly and freely and, therefore, are deserving of God's eternal wrath.

God has graciously made a way for humans to repent from sin and be forgiven (Acts 2:38; 3:19; Luke 24:47), but Scripture presents no such opportunity for Satan and the fallen angels. The decision to rebel against God or stay faithful to Him appears to have been an eternal choice for angels. Christian theology proposes that some angels—"the elect angels"—are those who remained loyal to God (1 Timothy 5:21). Other angels exercised their free will in rebellion and sinned against God (2 Peter 2:4). The Bible also seems to indicate that it is no longer possible for more of the angels to sin. It is as if all angels went through a type of probationary trial, and those who stayed true are now qualified to remain in their original state of perfect holiness. The elect angels successfully passed the test of faithfulness and are confirmed in holiness forever. The angels who failed and fell became "unclean spirits" or "demons" (Mark 1:23; Luke 8:2; 11:24 NKJV) and are now eternally confirmed in their evil, rebellious state.

In God's eyes, all sin is grievous. All sin impacts others. But the consequences are even more far-reaching for those who sin in high places. Satan and the angels had experienced God in all His heavenly glory. Those who sinned did so of their own volition and with full knowledge of their crime. Such heinous insurrection is unforgivable.

Satan's sin cost him his place in heaven. His example is a powerful reminder of the dangers of pride and rebellion. We have a choice to love God and obey Him. When we don't choose love of God, our decisions can have a profoundly detrimental influence on ourselves and those around us.

68. What does Satan look like?

The closest the Bible comes to describing what Satan and the demons look like is in 2 Corinthians 11:14, "Satan disguises himself as an angel of light" (ESV). The surrounding verses refer to Satan's human servants disguising themselves as "apostles of Christ" and "servants of righteousness." In context, these descriptions refer to false teachers. But the principle surely applies to demons as well.

One problem—and it's a big one—with trying to describe what Satan and demons look like is that *they are spirits*. Spirits are, by definition, nonphysical, and it is impossible to assign physical features to a nonphysical entity. As spirit beings, demons do not have noses, eyes, hands, feet, tails, or anything else that we might look for in drafting a description. That's one reason the Bible never describes Satan's appearance. Even the "angel of light" description in 2 Corinthians 11:14 is not meant as a sketch of his appearance; rather, it means to emphasize his deceitful nature. The devil wants us to believe he is truth when, in reality, he is falsehood.

Should Satan decide to make a physical appearance—if he manifested himself to us visibly—he would do so in a deceptive manner. The common, pop-culture portrayal of Satan as a scary, goat-like beast with horns is not found in the Bible. Prior to his rebellion against God, Satan was a beautiful, glorious being (see Ezekiel 28:12–15). What Satan "looks like" now is a mystery. Based on 2 Corinthians 11:14, though, we can know one thing for certain: Satan deceives people into thinking he is an angel of light. For Satan to reveal himself as the evil, murderous being that he is would be counterproductive. Most people would not follow the malicious maniac of conventional portrayals. Just as sin often looks attractive at first—only later revealing that it leads to death—so Satan would seek to deceive us by appearing as something other than evil.

The same is likely true of the demons. What do demons look like? No one in the Bible ever saw one outside of Micaiah's and John's divine visions; Micaiah did not provide visual details, and John, using apocalyptic symbolism, wrote of spirits "like frogs" (see 1 Kings 22:21–22 and Revelation 16:13). If demons were to take visible form, they would choose whatever would further their deception. As fallen angels, the demons are intelligent and powerful beings. And they are led by Satan, perhaps the most powerful created being (Jude 1:9). For demons to appear as evil beings would hinder their mission of deception and temptation.

What does Satan look like? What do demons look like? There is no way to know for certain. If they did appear, they would masquerade as something other than what they are. Deception wears a mask. Satan and the demons attempt to portray themselves as servants, guides, and "light" for people. But make no mistake, "the thief comes only to steal and kill and destroy" (John 10:10).

No matter what Satan would like us to think about himself, we know the truth: "Your enemy the devil prowls around like a roaring lion looking for someone to devour" (1 Peter 5:8). And we know his end: "The devil . . . was cast into the lake of fire and brimstone" (Revelation 20:10 NKJV).

69. Why did Satan think he could defeat God?

It is hard to imagine a being like Lucifer (Satan) believing he could even do battle with God, much less defeat Him. Even the most depraved mind should be able to see that a creature cannot possibly contend with the Creator. Yet Satan attempted to dethrone God and strives to this day to defy God's authority, thwart His plans, and harass His people.

Perhaps part of the explanation is that pride has blinded Satan to reality. Two Old Testament passages (Isaiah 14:12–15 and Ezekiel 28:11–19) discuss Satan's original position and the reasons for his loss of that position. Scripture tells of an exalted angelic being, one of God's creatures, who became proud. He determined to take the throne of God for himself. But God removed him from his position.

Satan's influence in worldly affairs is clearly revealed (John 12:31). Satan is extremely intelligent. Through his intelligence he deceived Adam and Eve and took over their rule of the world for himself (Genesis 1:26; 3:1–7; 2 Corinthians 11:3). His cleverness enables him to carry out his deceptive work almost at will, although his power is subject to God's restrictions (Job 1:12; Luke 4:6; 2 Thessalonians 2:7–8). He does have certain victories—although within the boundaries God has set for him—and perhaps these victories allow him to continue to delude himself that he can have victory over God.

The fact that God reins in Satan's activities is seen in Job, where Satan's freedom to afflict Job is curtailed (Job 1:7–12). Satan is permitted to trouble God's people (Luke 13:16; 1 Thessalonians 2:18; Hebrews 2:14) but never to win an ultimate victory over them (John 14:30–31; 16:33). A part of Satan's continuing ambition to replace God is his passionate yearning to have others worship him (Matthew 4:8–9; Revelation 13:4, 12). Satan is "the evil one" (Matthew 13:19, 38), while God is "the Holy One" (Isaiah 1:4).

Satan is destined to fail. His fate is predicted in John 12:31, Revelation 12:9, and 20:10. The death of Christ on the cross is the basis for Satan's final defeat (Hebrews 2:14–15; 1 Peter 3:18, 22). That event was the grand climax to a sinless life during which Jesus triumphed over the enemy repeatedly (Matthew 4:1–11; Luke 4:1–13). Satan probably rejoiced in the death of Christ, believing it to be a victory for him, but like all his victories, that one, too, was short-lived. When Jesus rose from the grave, Satan was once again defeated. The final victory will come when Jesus returns and Satan is cast into the lake of fire (Revelation 20:1–15).

The death and resurrection of Christ provide the believer strength for victory over sin. We have assurance that "the God of peace will soon crush Satan under your feet" (Romans 16:20). But such personal victory depends on God's grace and power in our lives and our will to offer resistance to Satan's temptations (Ephesians 4:25–27; James 4:7; 1 Peter 5:8–9). To help Christians win this battle against Satan, God has provided the power of Christ's blood (Revelation 12:11), the continuing prayer of Christ in heaven for believers (Hebrews 7:25), the leading of the Holy Spirit (Galatians 5:16), and armor for spiritual warfare (Ephesians 6:10–18).

70. Is Satan in hell?

At the moment, Satan is not in hell. Rather, Satan roams the earth, seeking people to tempt into sin and thus separate from God. First Peter 5:8 states, "Be alert and of sober mind. Your enemy the devil prowls around like a roaring lion looking for someone to devour."

In John 14:30, Jesus called Satan the "prince of this world," and the apostle Paul referred to him as the "ruler of the kingdom of the air, the spirit who is now at work in those who are disobedient" (Ephesians 2:2). Satan does not live in hell; he lives and works on the earth and in the heavens circling it.

Satan is the "father of lies" (John 8:44), and he influences and rules the world right now. Satan desires worship (Matthew 4:9), and he uses deceit and distractions to draw mankind's focus to himself. The world worships Satan in one way or another, except for those who are of the kingdom of God and are therefore called out of Satan's deceptions. If a person is not a child of God, he is by default a child of Satan (see John 8:44; Acts 13:10). First John 3:10 tells us how to distinguish the two: "This is how we know who the children of God are and who the children of the devil are: Anyone who does not do what is right is not God's child, nor is anyone who does not love their brother and sister." James 4:4 explains that anyone who is a friend of the world is an enemy of God.

This is important to know, because soon Jesus will return to earth and collect what belongs to Him. He will defeat the followers of Satan and claim His elect for Himself. Ultimately, Satan will be thrown into the lake of fire and "tormented day and night for ever and ever" (Revelation 20:10). Afterward, Jesus will judge unbelievers according to what they have done during their lives. Anyone whose name is not found written in the book of life is thrown into the lake of fire where Satan and his minions will be by that time (Revelation 20:10, 15). Hell and death are also thrown into the lake of fire (Revelation 20:14), so, technically speaking, at no time does Satan reside in hell. But he will be confined permanently in a very hot place that could be called a "hellish" location to be tormented eternally.

The key takeaway for each person is to ensure that his own name is written in the book of life so that he may have eternal life in heaven, rather than eternal separation from God in the lake of fire.

71. God vs. Satan—if God is all-powerful, why does He not just kill Satan?

One of the mysteries of the Christian life is why God didn't destroy Satan immediately after Satan sinned. We know that God will one day defeat Satan by throwing him into the lake of fire where he will be tortured day and night forever (Revelation 20:10), but sometimes we wonder why God has not destroyed Satan already. Perhaps we will never know God's exact reasoning, but we do know certain things about His nature.

First, we know God is sovereign over all creation, and this includes Satan. Certainly, Satan and his demons wreak havoc in the world, but they are only allowed a certain amount of freedom. We also know that God has planned everything from the beginning of time to the end. Nothing can thwart His plans, and things are proceeding exactly on schedule. "The LORD Almighty has sworn, 'Surely, as I have planned, so it will be, and as I have purposed, so it will happen'" (Isaiah 14:24).

Second, "we know that all things work together for good to those who love God, to those who are the called according to His purpose" (Romans 8:28 NKJV). God's plan to not immediately destroy Satan is the best plan possible. One day, God's perfect wrath and justice will be satisfied, and His perfect righteousness will be glorified. Those who love Him and who wait for His plan to be fulfilled will be thrilled to be part of that plan and will praise and glorify Him as they see it unfold.

Third, we know that to question God's plan and its timing is to question God Himself, His judgment, His character, and His very nature. God is both good and sovereign, and we can trust everything He does. The psalmist tells us, "As for God, his way is perfect" (Psalm 18:30). Whatever plan comes from the mind of the Almighty is the best plan possible. We can't expect to understand the mind of God perfectly, as He reminds us: "'For my thoughts are not your thoughts, neither are your ways my ways,' declares the LORD. 'As the heavens are higher than the earth, so are my ways higher than your ways and my thoughts than your thoughts'" (Isaiah 55:8–9). Nevertheless, our responsibility to God is to obey Him, trust Him, and submit to His will, regardless of how much we understand. We trust His timing for Satan's demise—God's plan is the best possible.

72. Was Satan the serpent in Genesis chapter 3?

Yes, the serpent in Genesis chapter 3 was Satan. Satan was either appearing as a serpent, possessing the serpent, or deceiving Adam and Eve into believing that it was the serpent that was talking to them. Serpents or snakes do not possess the ability to speak. Revelation 12:9 and 20:2 both describe Satan as "that ancient serpent," a term that seems to refer to his role as the tempter in Eden:

> The great dragon was hurled down—that ancient serpent called the devil, or Satan, who leads the whole world astray. He was hurled to the earth, and his angels with him.
>
> Revelation 12:9

> [An angel] seized the dragon, that ancient serpent, who is the devil, or Satan, and bound him for a thousand years.
>
> Revelation 20:2

The Bible does not say whether the serpent stood up or walked before the curse. If it was like other reptiles, it probably did walk on four legs. Some have suggested that the serpent may also have been able to fly, making its judgment even more dramatic. Some type of physiological change is apparent in Genesis 3:14: "So the LORD God said to the serpent, 'Because you have done this, Cursed are you above all livestock and all wild animals!

You will crawl on your belly and you will eat dust all the days of your life.'"

The fact that the serpent was cursed to crawl on its belly and "eat dust" also suggests that it would be forever despised. To this day, people tend to recoil from snakes as vile and contemptible creatures. The proverb "The only good snake is a dead snake" no doubt has its roots in the curse God pronounced on the serpent.

Why did God curse the serpent when it was actually Satan who led Adam and Eve into sin? Scripture does not say, but it could be that God chose to use the serpent as a constant reminder of Satan's fall and the result of sin. Every time we see a snake, we can be reminded that sin brings loss. The curse on the serpent doubled as a curse on Satan himself. Satan has already lost his position in heaven. And one day, in God's time, Satan "will be brought down to Sheol, to the recesses of the pit" (Isaiah 14:15, NASB; cf. Revelation 20:10; Ezekiel 28:18–19).

73. What are the names of Satan?

Satan is a powerful spiritual being who led a heavenly revolt against God and was subsequently cast down into the earth (Luke 10:18). His personal name, *Satan*, means "adversary." This name indicates Satan's basic nature: He is the enemy of God, of all God does, and of all God loves.

He is also called "the devil" in the New Testament. The word *devil* means "false accuser" or "slanderer." Satan plays this role in Job 1–2 when he attacks Job's character.

In Matthew 12:24, the Jews refer to Satan as "Beelzebul," an epithet derived from *Baal-Zebub* ("lord of the flies"), a false god of the Philistines in Ekron (2 Kings 1:2–3, 6).

Other titles of Satan include *tempter* (1 Thessalonians 3:5), *wicked one* (Matthew 13:19, 38 NKJV), and *accuser of our brethren* (Revelation 12:10 NKJV). Three additional titles point to Satan's present authority: *ruler of this world* (John 12:31 NKJV), *god of this age* (2 Corinthians 4:4), and *prince of the power of the air* (Ephesians 2:2 NKJV). As a deceiver and "the father of lies" (John 8:44), the devil "masquerades as an angel of light" (2 Corinthians 11:14).

There are a couple of passages that refer to the judgment of earthly kings but may very well also refer to Satan, the power behind those wicked kings. The first is Isaiah 14:12–15. This passage is addressed to the king of Babylon (v. 4), but the description also seems to fit that of a more powerful being. The name *Lucifer*, which means "morning star" or "light-bearer," is used here in several versions to describe a being who sought to overthrow God's very throne.

The second passage is Ezekiel 28:11–19, addressed to the king of Tyre. As in the Lucifer passage, this prophecy contains wording that seems to go beyond the description of a mere mortal. The king of Tyre is said to be "anointed as a guardian cherub" (Ezekiel 28:14), but he was laid low by pride and God Himself threw him to the earth (v. 17).

The Bible also uses various metaphors to reveal the character of our enemy, Satan. Jesus, in the parable of the four soils, likens Satan to the birds that snatch the seed off the hardened ground (Matthew 13:4, 19). In another parable, Satan appears as the sower of weeds among the wheat (Matthew 13:25, 28). Satan is analogous to a wolf in John 10:12 and a roaring lion in 1 Peter 5:8. In Revelation 12:9, Satan is the "great dragon . . . that ancient serpent"—a reference to the serpent that deceived Eve (Genesis 3:1).

74. Should Christians not capitalize the name *Satan*?

Capitalizing initial letters in pronouns related to God, such as *He* and *Him*, is a common tradition in English-speaking Christianity. Choosing this style is usually meant as a gesture of respect.

That leads some Christians to wonder about capitalizing the name *Satan* or titles such as *the devil.* If capitalizing a word is a form of showing respect, is it proper to capitalize the name of God's ultimate enemy? Is it better to write *Satan* in lowercase letters to indicate our disdain for him?

To answer, we should consider both accepted rules of writing and spiritual concerns. According to the rules of capitalization, proper names are capitalized. This would include the word *Satan,* or *Beelzebub,* as it is the devil's proper name. Titles such as *devil, evil one,* and *ruler of this world* require no capitalization.

In English, all proper nouns are capitalized, including names such as *John, Miguel,* and *Caoimhe.* The rule is not meant to venerate the person but to aid understandability and ease of reading. God's names are capitalized under that principle, and so is Satan's name. Modern English rules advise capitalizing Satan's name for that reason. Many modern, God-honoring translations of Scripture use entirely conventional capitalization: *Satan* is capitalized, not to show respect to the devil but to adhere to the rules of capitalization.

When it comes to pronouns, there is some flexibility. Pronouns referring to God may or may not be capitalized; it is a stylistic decision. It's quite common to see what's called "reverential capitalization" in the case of divine pronouns. Some Bible translations have chosen that route:

> Answer me, O Lord, for Your lovingkindness is good;
> According to the greatness of Your compassion, turn to me.
>
> Psalm 69:16 NASB1995

> When He had said this, He showed them His hands and His side.
>
> John 20:20 NKJV

Other translations have chosen to keep all pronouns lowercase, even those referring to deity:

> Answer me, O Lord, for your steadfast love is good;
> according to your abundant mercy, turn to me.
>
> Psalm 69:16 ESV

> When he had said this, he showed them his hands and his side.
>
> John 20:20 NET

Writers who use reverential capitalization do so to express their faith and honor the Lord. At the same time, there is nothing inherently disrespectful about using the lower case for all pronouns.

A frequently missed biblical teaching further supports using normal capitalization rules regarding *Satan*. At least twice, Scripture warns against belittling angelic beings (2 Peter 2:10–12; Jude 1:9–10). Even Michael the archangel did not slander the devil. To actively disrespect Satan—making a point to denigrate his name—touches on that problem. One could see it as taunting a powerful spiritual being. Further, to change the rules of capitalization concerning Satan's name could be a form of giving him special attention. It's better to treat his name according to the rules of common language rather than carve out a special exception for him.

We can rest assured that our enemy gets no reverence—and no provocation—when we stick to the conventional rules of capitalization. In the end, Christians are free to use whatever style suits their conscience (Romans 14:23); likewise, they should respect those with different views (Romans 14:1).

75. Does God love Satan?

No, God does not love Satan, and neither should we. God cannot love that which is evil and unholy, and Satan embodies all of that. He is the enemy (1 Peter 5:8); the evil one (Matthew 6:13); the father of lies and a murderer (John 8:44); the accuser of God's people (Revelation 12:10); the tempter (1 Thessalonians 3:5); proud, wicked, and violent (Ezekiel 28:16–18); a deceiver (Acts 13:10); a schemer (Ephesians 6:11); a thief (Luke 8:12); and many more evil things. He is, in fact, everything that God hates. The heart of Satan is fixed and confirmed in his hatred of God; his judgment is final, and his destruction is sure. Revelation 20 describes God's future plan for Satan, and love for Satan has no part in it.

Jesus' command that we love our enemies (Matthew 5:44) is meant to govern interpersonal relationships in this world. We love God, and we love people (even our enemies), who are made in God's image. Angels are not made in God's image. We are never told to love the holy angels, and we are certainly never told to love the evil angels.

Since Satan is everything that is antithetical to the God we love, we cannot love Satan. If we loved Satan, we would be forced to hate God, because holiness is the opposite of sin.

God has already determined that there will be no forgiveness for Satan; we are the objects of God's sacrificial love, shown on the cross. As God was lovingly redeeming mankind, He was putting Satan "to open shame" (Colossians 2:15 ESV). God's judgment of Satan will be part of His great love for us.

76. Why doesn't God forgive Satan?

In the early hours of October 16, 1946, ten condemned Nazi war criminals were hanged for crimes against humanity. None showed so much as a trace of remorse. No final regret or last-minute apology was uttered from the scaffold. On the contrary, one of them, Julius Streicher, whose incendiary attacks against Jews had fueled mob violence and anti-Semitic persecution, shouted, "Heil Hitler," as he ascended the steps to the platform where the hangman waited.[3] These ten were rebels to the end.

The higher the creature, the greater its capacity for evil. A madman can wreak more havoc than a mad dog, and a fallen angel more than an evil man. While Hitler and his unrepentant henchmen were guilty of plunging the world into a bloody, six-year war, Satan and his army of demons have been waging a full-scale attack against God and His people since the fall of mankind. All instances of suffering can be traced to Satan. His fingerprints can be found in every cemetery, prison, abortion clinic, crime scene, drug cartel, pornography studio, and wherever human degradation is found. He wields considerable influence in every nation's capital. He holds a seat in many corporate boardrooms. He serves as a regent in most of the world's colleges and universities. He knows his way around a movie set, a newspaper editorial board, a back-alley drug deal, and, regrettably, a growing number of church pulpits. Satan is relentless, and Scripture teaches he will be a rebel to the end.

Why doesn't God forgive Satan? Satan does not want God's forgiveness. He has no desire for divine mercy. Satan's singular goal is conquest; his chief ambition is to rule the whole of creation (Isaiah 14:12–14). His methods and ploys are many:

- He is the author of temptation (Genesis 3:1–5).
- He is the architect of evil works (1 John 3:8).
- He is a murderous liar (John 8:44).
- He inspires greed and dishonest gain (Acts 5:3).
- He falsely accuses God's people (Job 1; Zechariah 3:1–2).
- He is a vicious, well-armed combatant (Ephesians 6:11–16).
- He can enter into and possess the lost (Luke 22:1–6).
- He persecutes the saints (Revelation 2:10).
- He can perform supernatural signs and wonders (2 Thessalonians 2:9).

Based on the prophetic teachings of the Bible, the worst is yet to come. During a tumultuous time known as the seventieth week of Daniel (commonly referred to as the tribulation period), Satan will install a puppet ruler, the Antichrist, who will bring temporary peace and prosperity before showing his true colors (see Matthew 24; 2 Thessalonians 2:1–12; Revelation 13). Thankfully, Christ Jesus, our conquering hero, will defeat the Antichrist and put an end to his worldwide reign of terror. As for Satan, he will be bound and held captive during the Lord Jesus' one-thousand-year reign over the earth from His throne in Jerusalem (Revelation 20:1–6).

There have been human lawbreakers who repented of their crimes and became followers of Jesus Christ while in prison. The loss of one's liberties and the harsh realities of incarceration have motivated many to accept our Savior's forgiveness. Because of His boundless mercy, the Lord Jesus has never turned away a repentant sinner, regardless of the magnitude of his or her crime. Yet there are those who, like the Nazi war criminals, will resist the Lord until the bitter end. And Satan, even after a thousand years in chains, will refuse to wave the white flag of surrender; on the contrary, he will be eager to resume his battle against God and His people:

> And when the thousand years are ended, Satan will be released from his prison and will come out to deceive the nations that are at the four corners of the earth, Gog and Magog, to gather them for battle; their number is like the sand of the sea. And they marched up over the broad plain of the earth and surrounded the camp of the saints and the beloved city, but fire came down from heaven and consumed them, and the devil who had deceived them was thrown into the lake of fire and sulfur where the beast and the false prophet were, and they will be tormented day and night forever and ever.
>
> Revelation 20:7–10 ESV

Why doesn't God forgive Satan? One reason is that Satan will never repent. His heart is perpetually fixed on evil; he cannot be mended, only destroyed.

77. Why does God allow Satan to attack us?

Satan has a measure of control over the world (1 John 5:19), and he uses his power to attack us in various ways: (1) He stirs up fleshly lusts within us that tempt us to sin. (2) He attempts to deceive us with worldly "wisdom" opposed to God's truth. (3) He misleads us into a false gospel centered on a false Jesus. (4) He afflicts us physically with sickness, crime, tragedy, or persecution. Knowing that God is sovereign—Satan is not the ultimate ruler—we naturally ask, "Why does God allow Satan to attack us in these ways?"

The Bible teaches that God allows Satan a certain amount of freedom (see Job 1:12), but that freedom is always limited. Satan cannot do all that he wishes. Satan chooses to attack God's children (see 1 Peter 5:8), and his design is always evil. In contrast, God's design in allowing certain satanic attacks is always good; God loves His children (1 John 4:16). In the Old Testament, Joseph faced many satanic attacks in his lifetime, but in the end, he could speak with confidence of two opposing purposes behind the same events: "You [his brothers] intended to harm me, but God intended it for good" (Genesis 50:20).

We cannot blame God for what Satan does. Our vulnerability to satanic attack started with Adam's choice to follow Satan's lying suggestions in the Garden of Eden. When Satan attacked Job through the loss of his family, wealth, and health, Job was careful not to blame God. Notice Job 1:21–22, "And he [Job] said, 'Naked I came from my mother's womb, and naked shall I return. The LORD gave, and the LORD has taken away; blessed be the name of the LORD.' In all this Job did not sin or charge God with wrong" (ESV).

As believers experience the attacks of Satan, they can trust the truth of Romans 8:28, "We know that all things work together for good to those who love God" (NKJV). This verse suggests that we will experience both good and bad, but "all" things can be made to contribute toward good ends as God works them out. So, even the attacks of Satan, although evil in themselves, can and will work toward a good result. God can use our troubles, including attacks from Satan, to conform us to Christ (see Romans 8:29), increase our love, strengthen our faith, and produce patience along with many other virtues. Praise God for His sovereign protection through it all. Thank Him for His plan to make everything—even Satan's attacks—work together for our good!

78. When will Satan be defeated?

Satan. The devil. Beelzebul. Lucifer. He goes by many names, but the most powerful force of evil in the universe has already been defeated. The timer on the end of his evil activities was set when the Son of God walked out of the tomb (Matthew 28:7). Jesus defeated sin and death, and Satan was put on notice. Therefore, his time is short (see Revelation 12:12).

Satan's downfall began the moment he, as the angel Lucifer, challenged God and tried to redirect heaven's worship to himself (Isaiah 14:13–14). From the moment of his rebellion, Satan's doom was sure. God cast him from heaven to earth (Luke 10:18) where he tempted humanity into sin and caused Adam to follow his example and rebel against God (Genesis 3:6–7, 17–19; Romans 5:12). Satan is now called "the prince of the power of the air" (Ephesians 2:2 ESV), "the god of this world" (2 Corinthians 4:4 ESV), "the accuser" of Christians (Revelation 12:10), and "the deceiver of the whole world" (Revelation 12:9 ESV). God prepared hell as a place of punishment for Satan (Matthew 25:41).

One common misconception is that Satan and God are equal foes, battling for preeminence. This idea is completely false. God has no equal. He created all things, including the angel Lucifer, who became the being we call "Satan." As a created being, Satan only has the power and authority God gives him. We see this truth in the book of Job, where Satan has to ask permission to torment one of God's servants (Job 1:6–2:8). Jesus also alluded to Satan's short leash when He told His disciples that Satan had asked to test them (Luke 22:31–32). Satan's minions, the demons, must also ask the Lord's permission before they act (see Mark 5:9–13). For reasons known only to God, Satan is allowed to wreak havoc on the earth until the time when God will forever banish him.

First Corinthians 15:24–26 says, "Then the end will come, when [Jesus] hands over the kingdom to God the Father after he has destroyed all dominion, authority and power. For he must reign until he has put all his enemies under his feet. The last enemy to be destroyed is death." Satan's time of freedom is nearing the end. When Jesus returns, He will be victorious in a battle we call "Armageddon" (Revelation 16:16). It won't be much of a fight because Jesus annihilates Satan's forces with the word of His mouth (2 Thessalonians 2:8; Revelation 19:21).

After his defeat at Armageddon, Satan will be bound for a thousand years "to keep him from deceiving the nations anymore until the thousand years were ended. After that, he must be set free for a short time" (Revelation 20:3). At the end of that time, Satan is released; true to form, he leads one more rebellion against Christ and His kingdom (vv. 7–9). Again, Satan's forces are defeated, and Satan himself is "thrown into the lake of burning sulfur" to "be tormented day and night for ever and ever" (Revelation 20:10). After the final judgment of all those who have rejected Christ (Revelation 20:11–15), eternal paradise begins for the children of God. Sin and Satan are eternally banished.

In one sense, Satan is already defeated. Jesus won the victory over him through the cross and the resurrection (Colossians 2:15). It is now possible to live in victory over Satan every day of our lives. The Holy Spirit empowers God's children to say no to Satan's agenda and walk in the Spirit, living a life pleasing to

God (Ephesians 5:18; Galatians 5:16, 25). The ultimate defeat of Satan is yet to come, when he will be condemned to the lake of fire forever. His reign as the god of this world will be comparatively brief, and Christians can live in light of the truth that his doom is sure.

SECTION 10

Questions About Satan's Abilities

79. What did Jesus mean when He said, "I saw Satan fall like lightning from heaven," in Luke 10:18?

In Luke 10:18 Jesus says, "I saw Satan fall like lightning from heaven." The context of these words is the return of the seventy-two (or seventy, according to some manuscripts) disciples that Jesus had sent out to evangelize and prepare His way to Jerusalem (see v. 1). When the disciples return and give their report, they are joyful and a little surprised that "even the demons submit to us in your name" (v. 17). Jesus' first words in reply are, "I saw Satan fall like lightning from heaven" (v. 18).

In referencing Satan's fall from heaven, Jesus most likely spoke of the same event as Isaiah 14:12, "How you have fallen from heaven, morning star, son of the dawn! You have been cast down to the earth, you who once laid low the nations!" The fall of Satan that Jesus saw happened after Lucifer's sin, before Adam and Eve's temptation in the Garden of Eden. In his pride, Lucifer had lifted himself up, but God cast him down, and he lost his original place in heaven (although he retains a limited access to heaven for now, according to Job 1:6). Jesus' statement in Luke 10:18 speaks of Jesus' preexistence and the Lord's victory over the power of Satan in a general sense.

When Jesus' disciples came back to report their joy over their authority over demons, Jesus, in so many words, tells them they should not have been surprised. Satan is a fallen foe and has always been subject to the authority of the Son of God. Jesus had sent the seventy-two out in His authority, which extends over the demonic realm. Satan's fall "like lightning" indicates that his judgment in heaven was swift and obvious. Not only did Jesus give the disciples authority over devils, but He also enabled them "to trample on snakes and scorpions and to overcome all the power of the enemy" (Luke 10:19).

As these disciples are celebrating that the demons were subject to them in Jesus' name, Jesus redirects their excitement by pointing to an even bigger blessing: their salvation! Jesus says, "However, do not rejoice that the spirits submit to you, but rejoice that your names are written in heaven" (v. 20). Casting out demons has a temporal, limited benefit in this world, but having your name written in heaven is an eternal, unlimited blessing!

Revelation 12:9 refers to another time at which Satan is cast out of heaven: "The great dragon was hurled down—that ancient serpent called the devil, or Satan, who leads the whole world astray. He was hurled to the earth, and his angels with him." We believe this happens during the future tribulation period when Satan is barred access to heaven once and for all.

At the end of the great tribulation, Jesus will return and overthrow the kingdom Satan was attempting to set up, and the devil will be bound for one thousand years (Revelation 20:1–3). At the end of the thousand years, Satan will be released for one final battle, but he is defeated again and thrown into the lake of fire for eternity (Revelation 20:7–10).

Jesus has power over Satan and power to save us. Still today, believers face a spiritual battle against forces of evil (Ephesians 6:12). With God's Spirit, we do not need to fear Satan or evil spirits; rather, we depend on the Lord's strength for victory in our spiritual struggles and trust that God will preserve us for heaven's inheritance. "The one who is in you is greater than the one who is in the world" (1 John 4:4).

80. Why were Michael and Satan disputing over the body of Moses (Jude 1:9)?

Jude 1:9 refers to an event that is found nowhere else in Scripture. Michael the archangel had to struggle or dispute with Satan about the body of Moses. What that entailed and why it happened are not described. Was it an argument over possession of the body, the burial of the body, or something else?

A different angelic struggle is found in the book of Daniel. An angelic being rouses Daniel from a deep sleep (Daniel 10:7–11). The heavenly messenger tells Daniel that he was "resisted" by an entity called "the prince of the Persian kingdom" and that after twenty-one days, the archangel Michael came to the first angel's assistance (Daniel 10:13), allowing the angel to bring Daniel the message God wanted him to hear. So, we learn from Daniel that angels and demons fight spiritual battles and that the demons resist God's holy angels and try to prevent them from doing God's bidding.

Jude tells us that Michael the archangel contested Satan himself. Michael had been sent by God to deal in some way with the body of Moses. For the circumstances regarding Moses' death, see Deuteronomy 34:1–8.

Various theories have been put forth as to what this struggle over Moses' body was about. One is that Satan, ever the accuser of God's people (Revelation 12:10), may have resisted the raising of Moses to eternal life on the grounds of Moses' sin at Meribah (Deuteronomy 32:51) and his murder of the Egyptian (Exodus 2:12).

Some have supposed that Jude's reference is to the same event recorded in Zechariah 3:1–2: "Then he showed me Joshua the high priest standing before the angel of the LORD, and Satan standing at his right side to accuse him. The LORD said to Satan, 'The LORD rebuke you, Satan!'" But the only similarity between the two passages is the expression, "The Lord rebuke you." Also, the name *Michael* does not occur in the passage in Zechariah, and there is no mention of the body of Moses.

Some surmise that Jude is quoting a noncanonical book that contained this account and that Jude means to confirm that the account is true. Origen (ca. 185–254), an early Christian scholar and theologian, mentions a book called the Assumption of Moses as extant in his time, containing this very account of the contest between Michael and the devil. That book, now lost, is what Origen supposed was the source of the account in Jude.

The only material question, then, is whether the story of Michael's dispute with the devil is "true." Jude seems to refer to the confrontation as factual. He speaks of it the same way he would have spoken of the death of Moses or his smiting the rock. And, of course, no one can prove that it is *not* true. There are many allusions to angels in the Bible. The archangel Michael is real, and the devil is mentioned frequently in Scripture. There are numerous biblical affirmations of the existence of both bad and good angels, and some of their work on earth is detailed. Concerning the dispute over Moses' body, the nature and purpose of the incident is wholly unknown, making conjecture useless.

Jude 1:9 provides an example of how Christians are to deal with Satan and his demons. Michael's refusing to pronounce a curse upon Satan should be a lesson to Christians in how to relate to demonic forces. Believers are to seek the Lord's intervening power against the forces of darkness. If a being as powerful as Michael deferred to the Lord in dealing with Satan, who are we to attempt to reproach, insult, or command demons in our own strength?

81. Does Satan still have access to heaven?

Satan was originally one of God's holy angels, but he rebelled against God and was cast out of heaven (Luke 10:18). That was only the first stage of his judgment. Satan's kingdom was vanquished at the cross (John 12:31–32). In the future, he will be barred from all access to heaven (Revelation 12:7–9), bound in the Abyss for one thousand years (Revelation 20:1–3), and ultimately cast into the lake of fire for eternity (Revelation 20:10).

Until his final judgment, Satan is "the prince of this world" (John 14:30), but it seems that he still has restricted access to the heavenly realms. In Job 1:6, Satan stands in the presence of God. There is a similar situation in 2 Chronicles 18:18–21 involving a "deceiving spirit."

Since God is holy and absolutely without sin (Isaiah 6:3), and since He will not even look on evil (Habakkuk 1:13), how can Satan be in heaven? The answer involves God's sovereign restraint of sin. In Job 1, Satan stood before God to give an account of himself. God initiated the meeting, led the proceedings, and remained in absolute control (v. 7). The result was that Satan's power was limited (v. 12) and God was glorified.

Here are some other facts to note: (1) Satan does not have open access to God's presence. He is summoned by God. (2) The visits are temporary. His time before God's throne is limited. (3) In no way is the purity of heaven tainted by the brief, God-ordained presence of a sinful being, "quarantined," as it were, by God's regulatory power. And (4) Satan's access is only granted prior to the final judgment. After the judgment, God creates a new heaven and new earth (Revelation 21:1), wipes away all tears from our eyes (v. 4), reveals the New Jerusalem (v. 10), and promises the complete absence of sin (v. 27).

When we say, "God cannot allow sin into heaven," we simply mean that God cannot allow human beings who are still in their sin to live in His presence. But it is possible for God to command a sinful being to stand (temporarily) in His presence in order to commission him (see Isaiah 6), to exact an account from him (Job 1–2), or to judge him (Revelation 20:11–15) without compromising His holiness.

God's holiness will eventually consume all sin. Until that day, His holiness regulates sin, and that means that Satan, on certain occasions, is briefly summoned before his Creator to give an account of his actions.

82. Is Satan the master of hell?

There is a common misconception that Satan is in charge of hell and that he and his demons live there and use their pitchforks to torment souls for eternity. This concept has no basis in Scripture whatsoever. In fact, Satan will be one of the tormented in the lake of fire, not the tormentor (Revelation 20:10).

Where does the idea that Satan is the master of hell come from, if not from the Bible? Much of the false thinking may come from Dante Alighieri's *The Divine Comedy* and John Milton's *Paradise Lost*. Many other works of art and literary pieces follow Dante's lead and picture Satan as the one in charge of hell.

Dante's poem describes the brutal descent of sinners into the underworld. Dante journeys through different levels of hell and purgatory and eventually arrives in paradise. The poem itself was an amalgamation of myths, Catholic ideas (like purgatory), and Islamic traditions about Muhammad's "night of ascension" (*lailat al-miraj*). Dante's medieval view of hell is influenced more by the Qur'an than the Bible.

Dante's literary vision of hell is depicted by Botticelli in his painting *Map of Hell* as a subterranean funnel of suffering—a wretched underground landscape of fire, brimstone, sewage, and monsters, with Satan himself waiting at its core. It's all very disturbing, and effective as a work of art, but it is based on the imaginations of men, not the Word of God.

Satan is not the ruler of hell. It is God who is in charge. Jesus says, "Do not be afraid of those who kill the body and after that can do no more. . . . Fear him who, after your body has been killed, has authority to throw you into hell. Yes, I tell you, fear him" (Luke 12:4–5). Jesus is referring to God here. He alone has the power to throw someone into hell. Who holds the keys of death and Hades? Jesus has absolute control over that domain (Revelation 1:18).

The lake of fire, mentioned only in Revelation 19:20 and 20:10, 14–15, is the final place of punishment for all unrepentant rebels, both angelic and human (Matthew 25:41). The universal punishment for all who reject Jesus Christ as Savior is to be "thrown into the lake of fire" (Revelation 20:15). The Bible speaks of hell as a place of "outer darkness" where there will be "weeping and gnashing of teeth" (Matthew 8:12; 22:13 ESV). Those whose names are written in the Lamb's book of life should have no fear of this terrible fate. By faith in Christ and His shed blood, we are destined to live eternally in the presence of God.

Satan does not rule hell or lead his demons in tormenting those who are banished there. In fact, the Bible does not say that Satan has been to hell yet. Rather, "eternal fire" is awaiting Satan; the place was originally created to punish Satan and the demons (Matthew 25:41), not to give them a kingdom to rule.

Until Satan is condemned and thrown into the pit forever, he spends his time between heaven (Job 1:6–12) and earth (1 Peter 5:8). He will not always have freedom of movement, and he knows it. "Woe to the earth and the sea, because the devil has gone down to you! He is filled with fury, because he knows that his time is short" (Revelation 12:12).

83. How much power does Satan possess?

Satan was an angel created by God who turned against God's authority (Isaiah 14:13) and became the head of a kingdom of evil spirits called demons, his "angels" (Matthew 25:41). His power both in the heavenly realm and on earth is great and should not be underestimated. However, while Satan and his forces are formidable enemies, Jesus Christ crushed Satan's power, fulfilling the prophecy of Genesis 3:15. The cross of Christ won the victory (John 12:31). "The prince of this world now stands condemned" (John 16:11), and Jesus will one day destroy Satan's power completely and purify creation (2 Peter 3:10).

Satan's power in the heavenly realm/spirit world

Satan's power has repute in the spiritual realm (Jude 1:9), where he has limited access to the presence of God (Job 1:6). The book of Job provides insight into the relationship between God and Satan. In Job 1:6–12, Satan stands before God and reports that he has been "walking up and down" on the earth (v. 7 ESV). God asks Satan if he has considered godly Job, and Satan immediately accuses Job of insincerity—he only loves God for the blessings God gives. "Stretch out your hand," Satan says, "and strike everything he has, and he will surely curse you to your face" (v. 11). God grants Satan permission to affect Job's possessions and family but not his person, and Satan leaves. In Job 2, Satan comes again into God's presence and is, this time, permitted to affect Job's personal health. (The rest of the book is from Job's perspective, providing an example of how to deal with suffering.)

Job 1–2 is an important passage because it shows Satan's place in the spiritual realm. He is able to accuse God's people in His very presence, and Jude 1:9 shows that even Michael the archangel needs the Lord's help in overcoming Satan. However, Satan is obviously restrained from enacting his full fury; he is still a created being under God, and his power is limited.

Satan's power on the earth

Job 1 also reveals that Satan enacts evil and causes direct harm on the earth. The most far-reaching of his abysmal actions occurred in the Garden of Eden. Genesis 3 tells of Satan's temptation of Eve, the "mother of all the living" (v. 20), and her first sin. When Adam and Eve transgressed God's command, sin entered the world, and mankind lost their connection to life. That is why we must be redeemed from sin to have our fellowship with God restored.

During His earthly ministry, Jesus met a woman who had been "crippled by a spirit for eighteen years" (Luke 13:11). Jesus attributes the infirmity to Satan, who had kept her "bound" (v. 16). Satan's power was real, but it was easily overcome by our Lord: "He put his hands on her, and immediately she straightened up and praised God" (v. 13). Jesus' miracle was a clear demonstration of His authority over Satan.

Since his instigation of evil on earth, Satan has been named the "prince," "god," or "ruler" of this world (John 14:30; cf. John 12:31; 16:11; 2 Corinthians 4:3–4; Ephesians 2:2; Colossians 1:13). He is the enemy of God and truth (Matthew 13:24–30; 2 Thessalonians 2:9–12), and he does everything he can to tempt individuals (Genesis 3; Luke 22:31; 1 Timothy 3:7), groups (1 Thessalonians 3:5; Revelation 2:10), and nations. He "leads the whole world astray" (Revelation 12:9). Satan accomplishes this by various means, including appealing to man's pride (1 Timothy

3:6; 1 Corinthians 4:6), interfering with the transmission of truth (Matthew 13:18–22, 38–39), and placing false believers within the church (1 Timothy 4:1–2; 2 Timothy 3:1–9; Revelation 2:9; 3:9). Jesus called Satan "a liar and the father of lies" (John 8:44).

God still grants Satan some authority in this world, which means that his power is not yet completely broken—we still suffer from his attacks. But Hebrews 2:14 gives the good news that Jesus came to die in order to "break the power of him who holds the power of death—that is, the devil." The salvation Jesus provides releases us from Satan's stranglehold. Jesus is "the resurrection and the life. The one who believes in [Him] will live, even though they die" (John 11:25). Death has lost its sting (1 Corinthians 15:55).

Satan's power—the conclusion

The Bible says that "the whole world is under the control of the evil one" (1 John 5:19) and we must "be alert and of sober mind. Your enemy the devil prowls around like a roaring lion looking for someone to devour" (1 Peter 5:8). Yet Christians have a great hope, for Jesus Christ and our faith in Him have overcome Satan's evil (see 1 John 5:4). "The one who is in you is greater than the one who is in the world" (1 John 4:4).

84. What does the Bible say about demonic/satanic miracles?

Claims of religious miracles abound. Many Roman Catholics are convinced of the validity of various sightings of the Virgin Mary, stigmata, weeping or bleeding statues, and even "incorruptible bodies" that never decay after death. There are reported miracles in other religions, as well—Hinduism, Buddhism, and Islam all claim to have documented miracles.

Satan has the power to perform miracles. While his power is limited, he can and does perform miracles in order to deceive people. John 8:44 says that Satan is a liar and the father of lies. Satan can make himself appear as an angel of light (2 Corinthians 11:14). He does this to draw people away from God.

When Moses and Aaron confronted Pharaoh, they performed a miraculous sign to confirm their message from God (Exodus 7:8–10). The magi of Egypt were able to perform the same miracle "by their secret arts" (v. 11). God's miracle was shown to be greater (v. 12), but the fact is that the magi were able to perform a satanic miracle in the king's court.

During the tribulation, the Antichrist "will use all sorts of displays of power through signs and wonders that serve the lie" (2 Thessalonians 2:9). These miracles are explicitly said to be empowered by Satan. Jesus warned that the end times will be characterized by the treachery of counterfeit prophets who "will appear and perform great signs and wonders to deceive" (Matthew 24:24).

The fact of demonic miracles is one reason why we must test all spirits: "Dear friends, do not believe every spirit, but test the spirits to see whether they are from God, because many false prophets have gone out into the world" (1 John 4:1). Any time we are in doubt about a teaching, we are to make sure that it aligns with what Scripture says. If the miracle worker is teaching something contrary to God's Word, then his miracles, no matter how convincing they seem, are a demonic delusion.

Examples of convincing demonic miracles today are the apparitions of the Virgin Mary in different countries. These appearances of Mary seem legitimate; indeed, they are believed by millions of people. But when we compare what the apparitions say to what Scripture teaches, the lie becomes apparent. In various Marian apparitions, Mary supposedly said a church should be built in her honor (Our Lady of Guadalupe, 1531),[1] that God wants to establish worldwide devotion to Mary's immaculate heart (Fatima, 1917),[2] that she is the mediatrix between man and God (Fatima),[3] that "prayer and sacrifice" should be offered "in reparation to the Immaculate Heart of Mary to snatch souls from hell" (Fatima),[4] and that blessed objects should be worn in order to receive grace (Miraculous Medal, 1830).[5]

None of these messages are of God. Only Jesus can make reparation for our sin (1 John 2:2). Mary does not have an "immaculate" (sinless) heart. Devotion to Mary is not necessary, and Jesus is the only mediator between man and God (Hebrews 7:25; 1 Timothy 2:5; 1 John 2:1).

The message of the Marian apparitions clearly contradicts Scripture. Did the people who claim to have seen Mary experience a real miracle? Yes, possibly. However, the entity calling itself "Mary" is not working for God's glory or pointing people to Jesus Christ. Rather, Mary is being glorified, and people are being told to earn their own salvation by works.

Demonic miracles do occur. It is our responsibility to "be alert and of sober mind" (1 Peter 5:8) and not be fooled. We must keep our Bibles open, our heads clear, and our hearts fixed on Jesus.

85. Can Satan read our minds / know our thoughts?

First, it is important to remember that Satan is not omnipresent—he cannot be in more than one place at a time. Only God is everywhere, and only God knows everything. Satan is finite and does not know all things. He must rely on his army of demons to do his bidding.

Can Satan and/or his demons read our minds? No. First Kings 8:39 says that God alone knows every human heart. There is no one else who has that ability. God knows what we will say before we can say it, while the thought is still formulating (Psalm 139:4). Jesus, being God incarnate, exhibited the divine quality of knowing men's thoughts: "He knew what was in each person" (John 2:25; cf. Matthew 9:4; John 6:64).

The Bible does teach that Satan is powerful. Likely, he is the highest of all the fallen angels, and he was persuasive enough to convince one third of the angels to join him in his rebellion (see Revelation 12:4). Even after Satan's fall, not even Michael the archangel dared to rebuke him without the Lord's help (Jude 1:9). Satan is now the "the ruler of the kingdom of the air, the spirit who is now at work in those who are disobedient" (Ephesians 2:2). However, Satan's power has its limits, and reading our minds is beyond his ability.

Not being omniscient, Satan and his demons cannot read our minds. God is the only One who can know our thoughts. However, Satan and his demons have been observing and tempting human beings for thousands of years, and they know human nature better than any human. Even without the ability to know our thoughts, Satan can make analytic guesses as to what we are thinking and then tempt us accordingly. The order of commands in James 4:7 is important: The first is "Submit yourselves, then, to God," and the second is "Resist the devil." Above all else, we must guard our hearts (Proverbs 4:23).

86. Can Satan and/or his demons hear our prayers?

Prayer is speaking to God, and, as with any conversation, it is possible for others to overhear what we say. We assume that Satan can and does "eavesdrop" on our prayers—that is, he can hear what we pray about. This should not be of major concern to the child of God.

The Bible records many prayers from saints who prayed out loud, in their own language, with no fear that Satan might be eavesdropping:

Daniel: The law in Persia was that no one could petition any god except the king of Persia for thirty days, but that did not deter Daniel from praying. "He went home to his upstairs room where the windows opened toward Jerusalem. Three times a day he got down on his knees and prayed, giving thanks to his God, just as he had done before" (Daniel 6:10). Daniel's enemies were watching and probably eavesdropping. Satan might have been, too, but we aren't told. In any case, Daniel made no attempt to alter his prayer or to hide it from physical (or spiritual) eyes.

David: On the run from Saul, David prayed for the Lord's direction, and the Lord gave him a plan of escape (1 Samuel 23:9–14). If any situation ever called for concern that Satan might be eavesdropping, this was it. Yet David simply prayed, giving no thought to whether the devil heard.

Hezekiah: When King Hezekiah received a threatening letter from the Assyrians, "he went up to the temple of the LORD and spread [the letter] out before the LORD" (2 Kings 19:14). He then prayed for deliverance from the enemy. Satan is not mentioned at all in the passage, and we assume that Hezekiah did not care if Satan heard his prayer. He was praying to the Lord God Almighty, and that's all he cared about.

The early church: Publicly and audibly, the church in Jerusalem "raised their voices together in prayer to God" (Acts 4:24). They praised the Lord, cited Scripture, and asked for boldness and power (vv. 24–30). They showed no concern whatsoever about who else or what else might hear them.

The above cases have at least two things in common:

1. Satan is not mentioned even once.
2. Those who prayed simply talked to God in a heartfelt, straightforward manner.
3. The prayer was answered.

As they prayed, Daniel, David, Hezekiah, and the Jerusalem church focused on God and God alone. If the thought that Satan was listening ever crossed their minds—and it doesn't seem that it did—their attitude would likely have been, "So what?" Satan might hear us—so what? The devil will do his worst—so what? We're not talking to *him*; we're talking to the Sovereign God of the universe! Our God will hear our cry and act on our behalf, regardless of what Satan hears or doesn't hear, or what he does or doesn't do.

Satan can eavesdrop if he wants, but he is not stronger than the Holy Spirit, who "prays for us with groanings that cannot be expressed in words. And the Father who knows all hearts knows what the Spirit is saying, for the Spirit pleads for us believers in harmony with God's own will" (Romans 8:26–27 NLT).

Satan and his demonic hordes have absolutely no power to prevent God from answering our prayers according to His will. So, there is no need to stop verbalizing our prayers to keep Satan from hearing them. And there is no need to employ a "heavenly language" to try to "fool" Satan. God hears, and that's all that matters. Whether Satan and his demons hear and understand our prayers is irrelevant.

SECTION 11

Questions About Us and Demons

87. Is there activity of demonic spirits in the world today?

Ghosts, hauntings, séances, tarot cards, Ouija boards, crystal balls—what do they have in common? They are fascinating to many people because they seem to offer insight into an unknown world that lies beyond the limits of our physical existence. And to many, such things seem innocent and harmless.

Many who approach these subjects from nonbiblical perspectives believe that ghosts are the spirits of dead people who, for whatever reason, have not gone on to the "next stage." According to those who believe in ghosts, there are three different kinds of hauntings: (1) Residual hauntings, which are likened to video recordings of past, high-energy events; residual hauntings do not feature personal interaction with spirits, but witnesses may hear the sound of footsteps in a hallway, see a shadowy figure in a window, or hear snippets of bygone conversations. (2) Hauntings by human spirits, whose natures are a combination of good and bad (but not evil). Such spirits may simply want to get a person's attention; others may be pranksters, but, in either case, they do not truly harm people. (3) Interaction with nonhuman spirits or demons. These entities can masquerade as human spirits, but they are harmful and dangerous.

When reading about ghosts and hauntings from nonbiblical sources, remember that, just because an author may refer to the Bible or to Bible characters (such as Michael the archangel), it does not mean he approaches the subject from a biblical perspective. When no authority is given for an author's information, the reader has to ask, "How does the author know this to be so? What is his or her authority?" For example, how does an author know that demons masquerade as human spirits? Ultimately, those who address such subjects from nonbiblical sources must base their understanding on their own thoughts, the thoughts of others, and/or historical experiences. Of course, an author who admits that demons are deceitful must allow that experiences can be untrustworthy! To have a right understanding on this subject, we must go to a source that has shown itself to be accurate 100 percent of the time—God's Word, the Bible. Let's look at what the Bible has to say about such things.

1. The Bible never speaks of hauntings. Rather, it teaches that, when a person dies, the spirit of that person goes to one of two places. If the person is a believer in Jesus Christ, his spirit is ushered into the presence of the Lord in heaven (Philippians 1:21–23; 2 Corinthians 5:8). Later, he will be reunited with his body at the resurrection (1 Thessalonians 4:13–18). If the person is not a believer

in Christ, his spirit goes to a place of torment called hell (Luke 16:23–24).

Whether a person is a believer or an unbeliever, there is no returning to our world to communicate or interact with people, even for the purpose of warning people to flee from the judgment to come (see Luke 16:27–31). There are only two recorded incidents in which a dead person interacted with the living. The first is when King Saul of Israel tried contacting the deceased prophet Samuel through a medium. God allowed Samuel to be disturbed long enough to pronounce judgment upon Saul for his repeated disobedience (1 Samuel 28:6–19). The second incident is when Moses and Elijah interacted with Jesus when the Lord was transfigured (Matthew 17:1–8). There was nothing "ghostly" about the appearance of Moses and Elijah, however.

2. Scripture speaks repeatedly of angels moving about unseen (Daniel 10:1–21). Sometimes, these angels interact with living people. Evil spirits, or demons, can actually possess people, dwelling within them and controlling them (see Mark 5:1–20, for example). The four Gospels and the book of Acts record several instances of demon possession and of good angels appearing to and aiding believers. Angels, both good and bad, can cause supernatural phenomena to occur (Job 1–2; Revelation 7:1; 8:5; 15:1; 16).
3. Scripture shows that demons know things of which people are unaware (Acts 16:16–18; Luke 4:41). Because these evil angels have been around a long time, they would naturally know things that those with limited lifespans would not. Because Satan currently has access to God's presence (Job 1—2), demons might also be allowed to know some things about the future, but this is speculation.

4. Scripture says Satan is the father of lies and a deceiver (John 8:44; 2 Thessalonians 2:9) and that he disguises himself as an "angel of light" (2 Corinthians 11:14). Those who follow him practice the same deceit (2 Corinthians 11:13–15).
5. Satan and demons have great power (compared with humans). Even Michael the archangel trusts only God's power when dealing with Satan (Jude 1:9). But Satan's power is nothing compared with God's (Acts 19:11–12; Mark 5:1–20), and God is able to use Satan's evil intent to bring about His own good purposes (1 Corinthians 5:5; 2 Corinthians 12:7).
6. God commands us to have nothing to do with the occult, devil worship, or the unclean spirit world. This would include the use of mediums, séances, Ouija boards, horoscopes, tarot cards, channeling, etc. God considers these practices an abomination (Deuteronomy 18:9–12; Isaiah 8:19–20; Galatians 5:20; Revelation 21:8), and those who involve themselves in such things invite disaster (Acts 19:13–16).
7. The Ephesian believers set an example in dealing with occult items (books, music, jewelry, games, etc.). They confessed their involvement with such things as sin and burned the items publicly (Acts 19:17–19).
8. Release from Satan's power is achieved through God's salvation. Salvation comes through believing in the gospel of Jesus Christ (Acts 19:18; 26:16–18). Attempts to disentangle oneself from demonic involvement without salvation are futile. Jesus warned of a heart devoid of the Holy Spirit's presence: Such a heart is merely an empty dwelling place ready for even worse demons to inhabit (Luke 11:24–26). But when a person comes to Christ for the forgiveness of sin, the Holy Spirit comes to abide until the day of redemption (Ephesians 4:30).

Some paranormal activity can be attributed to the work of charlatans. It would seem best to understand other reports of ghosts and hauntings as the work of demons. Sometimes these demons may make no attempt to conceal their nature; other times they may use deception, appearing as spirits of the departed. Such deception leads to more lies and confusion.

God states it is foolish to consult the dead on behalf of the living. Rather, God's people are to go "to the law and to the testimony!" (Isaiah 8:20 NKJV). The Word of God is our source of wisdom. Believers in Jesus Christ should not be involved in the occult. The spirit world is real, but Christians do not need to fear it (1 John 4:4).

88. Is seeing spirits/demons an ability God gives to some people?

There are some who believe they have the ability to see spirits, ghosts, angels, demons, etc. Online advice on what to do with this gift abounds, and books, including children's books, purport to help people use their gift. But despite those who claim to see spirits, the Bible says nothing about such a gift or ability.

The Bible records instances of spirits manifesting themselves visibly. The Holy Spirit Himself appeared as a dove in Matthew 3:16 and as a flame of fire in Acts 2:3. Holy angels have manifested themselves to people, but in almost every case it is the angel who takes the initiative to reveal himself; he is not seen because someone had the "gift" of special sight. An exception is 2 Kings 6:17, when Elisha prays for his servant's eyes to be opened to the spiritual reality around him, but even then, the servant had no permanent gift or innate ability to see the angels. There is no biblical record of an evil spirit manifesting or being seen.

Some biblical prophets had visions of God and angels, and angels sometimes appeared to people in dreams. But receiving a vision in the course of a prophet's duties is different from a native ability to see spirits. The occasional glimpses of the spirit world had by prophets and others were allowed by God for His own purposes. A biblical seer was not a person who could see angels but someone through whom God's word came.

In all the times that the Bible records people seeing spiritual beings, there is never a mention of any special "gift" or "ability" associated with such sights. Christians who are trusting God can be sure that angels are all around us doing what they do behind the scenes. We don't need to physically see angels to understand that they are there.

King Saul used a medium to summon the spirit of Samuel so that he could ask Samuel's advice (1 Samuel 28). The woman obliged but then reacted in fear and "cried out at the top of her voice" when Samuel really did appear (1 Samuel 28:12). Her terrified response showed that she did not usually get that kind of result. There are mediums today who claim to be able to communicate with spirits. Some may be charlatans, but some may actually receive communication from the spirit world. Whether they can *see* spirits is another matter; the manifestation of Samuel's spirit to Saul's medium seems to be a unique instance in Scripture.

God condemns any communication with the dead. Saul was judged for his actions regarding the medium: "Saul died because he was unfaithful to the LORD; he did not keep the word of the LORD and even consulted a medium for guidance, and did not inquire of the LORD. So the LORD put him to death and turned the kingdom over to David son of Jesse" (1 Chronicles 10:13–14). Furthermore, the New Testament warns that Satan masquerades as an angel of light in order to deceive (2 Corinthians 11:14). Christians should seek guidance from the Lord and from His Word, not from departed spirits.

People who claim a gift of seeing angels or demons or to possess some type of extrasensory perception are functioning apart from Scripture. The Bible gives no indication that God gives such a gift or ability to people, and Scripture must be our final authority in spiritual matters.

89. What does the Bible say about casting out demons?

The Bible affirms the reality of demons—fallen angels who oppose God and seek to harm His creation (Revelation 12:9). Throughout Scripture, we see instances of demonic possession and oppression, and we also see God's power triumphing over these forces. Jesus Himself frequently cast out demons during His earthly ministry, demonstrating His authority over the spiritual realm. One example is in Mark 1:34: "Jesus healed many who had various diseases. He also drove out many demons, but he would not let the demons speak because they knew who he was." This shows that Jesus had complete control over demonic forces and silenced them at will.

Jesus also gave His disciples authority to cast out demons. In Luke 10:17, the seventy-two (or seventy) disciples returned from their mission with joy, saying, "Lord, even the demons submit to us in your name." However, Jesus reminded them in Luke 10:20, "Do not rejoice that the spirits submit to you, but rejoice that your names are written in heaven." So, the power to cast out demons is not something to boast in. The greatest gift someone can have is not power over demons but eternal salvation.

The early church also encountered demonic activity, and there were demons cast out during the apostolic age. In Acts 16:18, Paul cast a spirit of divination out of a slave girl by saying, "In the name of Jesus Christ I command you to come out of her!" The demon left her immediately. This passage, along with others, shows that the authority to cast out demons comes not from human power or some type of ritual, but from the name and authority of Jesus Christ.

It's important to note that the Bible never commands believers to perform exorcisms, nor does it present exorcism as a common or routine practice for Christians. The ability to cast out demons was part of the apostolic ministry and served to authenticate the message of the gospel in the first century. While God can and does still deliver people from demonic oppression today, the Bible does not instruct Christians to seek out demons in order to engage them in confrontational spiritual warfare. In fact, Jude 1:9 gives a sobering example of the humility we need in this matter: "Even the archangel Michael, when he was disputing with the devil about the body of Moses, did not himself dare to condemn him for slander but said, 'The Lord rebuke you!'" Even Michael the archangel did not rebuke Satan directly but appealed to the Lord's authority.

Christians are called to resist the devil, not to engage him directly. James 4:7 says, "Submit yourselves, then, to God. Resist the devil, and he will flee from you." Our focus should be on submitting to God, living in obedience to Christ, and standing firm in faith. While demonic activity is real, the Bible emphasizes the believer's security in Christ and the sufficiency of God's power to protect and deliver. As 1 John 4:4 reminds us, "The one who is in you is greater than the one who is in the world."

We believe that casting out demons is biblical, in the sense that it occurred in several historical events recorded in Scripture. The ability to cast out demons was given to the Twelve and to the seventy-two, but there is no blanket gift of exorcism given today, in the post-apostolic era. Our responsibility is to "put on the full armor of God, so that when the day of evil comes, [we] may be able to stand [our] ground, and after [we] have done everything, to stand" (Ephesians 6:13).

90. How do we distinguish a psychological disorder from demon possession?

The short answer to this question is that the Bible does not address how to distinguish between demon possession and a psychological disorder. Because God chose not to equip Christians for this task, we should probably assume this is not something we are called to do. However, there are two related truths we know for sure from Scripture:

First, demons can possess those who do not belong to Christ, and Scripture gives some examples of people being possessed by demons. From the biblical descriptions, we can identify some symptoms of demonic influence and gain insight about how a demon possesses someone. In some of these passages (e.g., Matthew 9:32–33; Mark 9:17–18), the demon possession causes physical ailments—inability to speak, epileptic symptoms, blindness, etc. In other cases, the demon causes the individual to perform evil acts (Judas is an example). In Acts 16:16–18, a "spirit of divination" (ESV) apparently gave a slave girl some ability to know things beyond her own learning. In the case of the demoniac of the Gerasenes, who was possessed by a multitude of demons, the demons gave the man superhuman strength and caused him to cut himself and live naked among the tombstones (Mark 5:1–17). King Saul, after rebelling against the Lord, was troubled by an evil spirit (1 Samuel 16:14–15; 18:10–11; 19:9–10) with the apparent effect of a melancholy mood and an increased desire and readiness to kill David, God's next anointed king of Israel.

Second, it is impossible for a Christian to be possessed by a demon. The believer is indwelt by the Holy Spirit of God who comes to reside in our hearts when we give our lives to Christ (2 Corinthians 1:22). Biblical descriptions of demons identify them as "evil," "unclean," or "impure" (see Mark 5:2). The Holy Spirit cannot possibly share His dwelling place with such a creature. For those who do not have the Holy Spirit, however, no amount of good living or "cleaning up their act" will prevent a demon from possessing or influencing them. The parable Jesus told in Matthew 12:43–45 (NKJV) makes this clear:

> When an unclean spirit goes out of a man, he goes through dry places, seeking rest, and finds none. Then he says, "I will return to my house from which I came." And when he comes, he finds it empty, swept, and put in order. Then he goes and takes with him seven other spirits more wicked than himself, and they enter and dwell there; and the last state of that man is worse than the first.

In giving this parable, Jesus was denouncing the unbelief of Israel, but the illustration He uses gives some insight into the behavior of demons. Unclean spirits seek to take up residence in people, and, on their own, people are powerless to stop them. Any type of self-improvement or personal reformation apart from Christ is futile in barring the door against the devil. In the words of commentator Matthew Poole, "Reformation proves but a sweeping and a garnishing, while the soul is empty of Christ. It may be swept from the filth of flagitious sins, and garnished with the paint of religion, or some habits of moral virtue; but none of these will keep out the devil."[1] We must be born again (John 3:3; cf. Ezekiel 36:26). We need new life in Christ (2 Corinthians 5:17). We need the indwelling Holy Spirit, for then "He who is in you is greater than he who is in the world" (1 John 4:4 NKJV).

While Christians cannot be possessed by a demon, they can still be influenced by one. The apostle Peter was one of Christ's closest three disciples, yet he was influenced by the devil (Matthew 16:23). We must keep our armor on (see Ephesians 6:10–17). We must, as Peter said, "be alert and of sober mind. Your enemy the devil prowls around like a roaring lion looking for someone to devour" (1 Peter 5:8).

A word to the wise: Do not allow yourself to develop an unhealthy fascination with the occult and demonic activity. Scripture informs us of what we need to know about demons. If we do need to discern between demonic possession and a psychological disorder, we can pray for wisdom. God promises that "he will give it to you. He will not rebuke you for asking" (James 1:5 NLT).

91. Can Christians be demon possessed?

The Bible does not explicitly state whether a Christian can be possessed by a demon, but related biblical truths indicate that, no, believers cannot be demon possessed.

A quick defining of terms is appropriate here: demon *possession* is the state of being indwelt by a demon who has direct control over the thoughts and/or actions of a person (Matthew 17:14–18; Luke 4:33–35; 8:27–33). The man Jesus met in the region of the Gesarenes was demon possessed. Demon *oppression* or *influence* involves a demonic attack on a person from without. Oppression can result in spiritual and/or physical trouble and strong temptation to sin. Job was oppressed by Satan.

A believer in Jesus Christ is born again to be a new creation and a child of God. As such, he or she is indwelt by the Holy Spirit, baptized into the body of Christ, seated in heavenly places, and served by angels. The Christian has been chosen by God, bought with the blood of Christ, and sealed by the Spirit. God's children are "a chosen race, a royal priesthood, a holy nation" (1 Peter 2:9 ESV). They belong to God, and Jesus is their Shepherd (see John 1:12; 10:14, 28–30; Romans 8:9–11, 15; 1 Corinthians 3:16; 6:19; 12:13; Ephesians 1:13; 2:6; Hebrews 1:14.) Given these truths, there is no way possible for a follower of Christ to be demon possessed.

The Holy Spirit would not allow a demon to possess the same person He is indwelling. The Holy One will not share space with the wicked one. Satan is undoubtedly powerful—he is the "strong man" in Jesus' parable in Mark 3. But Jesus is the One who "binds the strong man" and takes possession of "his house" when a person is born again (Mark 3:27 NKJV). The strong man is feeble and defenseless in the presence of the Spirit of Christ. The believer need not fear that the devil will regain control.

Scripture declares, "You, dear children, are from God and have overcome [false teachers], because the one who is in you is greater than the one who is in the world" (1 John 4:4). Who is the One in us? The Holy Spirit. Who is the one in the world? Satan and, by extension, his demons. This is good news: The believer has overcome the world of demons, with all their falsehood and deception.

The biblical evidence that a Christian *cannot* be demon possessed is strong. That's why some Bible teachers use the term *demonization* to refer to a demon having control over a Christian. They argue that, while a Christian cannot be demon possessed, a Christian can be "demonized." Typically, the description of demonization is virtually identical to that of demon possession. But changing the terminology does not change the fact that a demon cannot inhabit or take control of a Christian. Demonic influence and oppression are realities for Christians, but it is not biblical to say that a Christian can be possessed by a demon or demonized.

Much of the reasoning behind the concept of demonization is based on a misinterpretation of personal experience. So, someone who is "definitely" a Christian begins to exhibit evidence of being controlled by a demon, and that is taken as "proof" of demonization. At this point, it's important not to allow personal experience to color our interpretation of Scripture. Personal experience plays a secondary role to the truth of Scripture (2 Timothy 3:16–17). Seeing someone whom we thought was a Christian exhibiting behavior associated with demon possession should cause us to question the genuineness of the faith of that person. Judas Iscariot was indwelt by Satan (John 13:27), but Judas, according to Jesus, was not truly one of His—he was "a devil" (John 6:70). Perhaps the person truly is a Christian but is severely demon oppressed and/or suffering from acute psychological problems. But a Christian cannot be demon possessed/demonized. The Holy Spirit has not rented out space to an unholy spirit.

92. What does the Bible say about demonic oppression?

There is strong biblical evidence that a Christian cannot be demon possessed. But the question remains about how much influence a demon can have over a Christian. Many Bible teachers describe demonic influence on a Christian as "demonic oppression" to distinguish it from possession.

When a demon possesses a person, it enters that person and has direct control over the person's mind and body (see Matthew 17:14–18; Luke 4:33–35; 8:27–33). Demonic oppression, on the other hand, involves an external demonic attack. Oppression can result in spiritual and/or physical trouble and strong temptation to sin.

The Bible says that the devil seeks to devour believers (1 Peter 5:8), and Satan and his demons carry out "schemes" against Christians (Ephesians 6:11). As Satan tempted Jesus (Luke 4:2), so demonic forces tempt us to sin. A believer being oppressed by demons will often experience strong temptation, feelings of despair and doubt, and, in some instances, physical ailments. The Christian under attack will be hindered in his ability to serve God and might even give in to the temptation. At the point of stumbling, the oppression can increase to the extent that the demon strongly influences the Christian's thoughts and behavior.

Job was a godly man, yet he was severely oppressed by Satan. Peter was one of Jesus' closest disciples, yet he also experienced demonic oppression. Jesus warned him ahead of time: "Simon, Simon, Satan has asked to sift all of you as wheat. But I have prayed for you, Simon, that your faith may not fail. And when you have turned back, strengthen your brothers" (Luke 22:31–32). Later that same night, Peter denied the Lord three times. The devil seemed to have won a victory, but the Lord had promised that Peter would return and be able to strengthen others.

When we are oppressed by our spiritual enemies, we must turn to God for help: "The name of the LORD is a fortified tower; the righteous run to it and are safe" (Proverbs 18:10). God alone can break the power of demonic influence. He will rescue His children: "This poor man called, and the LORD heard him; he saved him out of all his troubles" (Psalm 34:6). The apostle John gives us great encouragement in this area: "We know that anyone born of God does not continue to sin; the One who was born of God keeps them safe, and the evil one cannot harm them" (1 John 5:18).

Victory over demonic oppression is always available to the Christian. John declares, "The one who is in you is greater than the one who is in the world" (1 John 4:4). We have the indwelling Holy Spirit, and nothing, "neither angels nor demons," can separate us from the love of God in Christ (Romans 8:38–39).

Peter encourages believers to resist the devil, "standing firm in the faith" (1 Peter 5:9). We must rely on the power of the Holy Spirit to successfully fight against demonic oppression. We must build our faith through the Word of God, persistent prayer, and godly fellowship with other believers. Our faith is a shield with which we can "extinguish all the flaming arrows of the evil one" (Ephesians 6:16).

93. How much emphasis should be given to demonic deliverance in the Christian life?

There are two extremes in people's thinking about demons. One says that there is nothing supernatural about "demons" and that what we call demons are nothing more than negative thoughts or behaviors. Those who hold this view believe that deliverance from a "demon" comes through counseling, medical intervention, or a twelve-step program. The other extreme says that anything negative is the work of evil spirits or demons. Those who hold this view often "rebuke" everything from a common cold to inconvenient rainfall to a drop in the stock market. The correct emphasis on demonic deliverance lies somewhere between these two extremes.

Demons are fallen spiritual beings. They are real, and they interfere in human affairs (Matthew 12:43; Mark 1:26; Acts 8:7). Scripture is matter-of-fact in its presentation of demons and their evil work—a work that continues to this day (see 1 Peter 5:8). It would be an error, however, to overemphasize the work of Satan. We should not give him more attention than he deserves. Our focus should be on the glory of God and His righteousness (Matthew 6:33), since "the one who is in you is greater than the one who is in the world" (1 John 4:4). Satan and God are not "equal" or "balanced" opposites, in a yin-yang way. Satan is a created, finite being who possesses only the power God allows him to have (see Job 1:9–10).

Jesus cast out many demons during His earthly ministry, and the early church continued to address spiritual warfare after Jesus had ascended back to heaven (Acts 5:3; 8:7; Ephesians 6:11–13; 2 Corinthians 10:3–5). There is no evidence to suggest that Satan and his fallen angels have ceased to torment human beings. However, James 1:13–15 teaches that much of our struggle against sin is due to our own fleshly desires, not a direct attack from Satan.

A Christian cannot be demon possessed, but he or she can suffer demonic oppression. Satan can still wreak a great deal of havoc in our lives. He cannot steal the soul of a Christian or snatch him away from God's hand (John 10:29), but he can render the believer fruitless and rob his life of joy.

Ephesians 6:10–17 instructs us in combating the forces of darkness. We are told to continually put on the "full armor of God" (v. 11) and "stand firm" (v. 14). Although Satan and his forces are constantly at work to "steal and kill and destroy" (John 10:10), God has given His children all they need to be victorious against spiritual attacks. We are told to resist the devil (James 4:7), be wary of him (1 Peter 5:8), and not give him room in our lives (Ephesians 4:27).

When a believer needs to be delivered from satanic attacks, he or she must call on the Lord. God will rescue His children in their time of need: "The Lord is faithful, and he will strengthen you and protect you from the evil one" (2 Thessalonians 3:3). We can pray confidently with David,

> I say to the LORD, "You are my God."
> Hear, LORD, my cry for mercy.
> Sovereign LORD, my strong deliverer,
> you shield my head in the day of battle.
> Do not grant the wicked their desires, LORD;
> do not let their plans succeed.
>
> Psalm 140:6–8

When Jesus was tempted by Satan (Luke 4:1–12), He used the "sword of the Spirit, which is the word of God" (Ephesians 6:17) to rebuke His enemy. Every time Satan came against Him, He replied, "It is written. . . ," and He applied Scripture to His situation. The best defense against demonic attack is the Word of God.

Christians are in a spiritual battle, and we need to be aware of the spiritual realities we face. But we do not need to look for demons everywhere; our focus should not be on demons but "on Jesus, the pioneer and perfecter of faith" (Hebrews 12:2). That's where the victory is.

94. How does Satan tempt us?

Satan and his demons are constantly tempting human beings to sin against God, and the Bible gives us many examples. The devil "prowls around like a roaring lion looking for someone to devour" (1 Peter 5:8). Satan fills people's hearts with lies (Acts 5:3). He is "the tempter" (1 Thessalonians 3:5).

In Satan's temptation of Eve in Genesis 3 and in his temptation of Jesus in Matthew 4, we see the tactics he used and still uses with us. While varied in their details, most temptations fall into one of three categories listed in 1 John 2:16: the lust of the flesh, the lust of the eyes, and the pride of life.

In Satan's first temptation of Jesus, he appealed to the lust of the flesh. Jesus was hungry, and Satan tempted Him to use His power to make bread for Himself (Matthew 4:1–3). Jesus resisted the temptation, but the encounter shows that Satan does not play fair. He exploits our physical weaknesses and kicks us when we're down. He knows the weak places in our flesh and looks for opportunities to stir illicit passions inside our hearts.

When Satan tempted Eve to eat the forbidden fruit, he suggested that the Lord was keeping something from her that "was good for food" (Genesis 3:6). When he tempts us with the lust of the flesh, he points to a natural desire and suggests that we should meet it in our own selfish way. Eve's natural desire for food was not wrong, but Satan exploited it. That desire became sin when she fulfilled it in an ungodly way. The same principle often leads to sexual immorality, which begins with a natural desire for intimacy. But, if we have not allowed Jesus to become a greater passion, the tempter may convince us that we should meet the need for intimacy our own way.

The second way Satan tempts us is through the lust of the eyes. Eve's eyes rebelled against God's commandment when she "saw that the fruit of the tree was . . . pleasing to the eye" (Genesis 3:6). Our eyes play a major role in our decision-making. We see something we want, and our flesh agrees that we must have it. In this age of visual overstimulation, our eyes take in millions of bits of information through the day, and, unless we filter that information through a pure heart (Matthew 5:8; Psalm 24:4), our eyes will lead us into sin.

Samson's downhill slide started with the lust of the eyes. Judges 14–16 details Samson's flirtation with sin and the tragic results. As God's chosen leader, Samson had no business hanging out in Philistine territory, much less flirting with their women. But his eyes led him into sin: "Then Samson went down to Timnah and *saw* . . . one of the daughters of the Philistines. So he came back and told his father and mother, '*I saw* a woman. . . . Get her for me, for *she looks good to me*'" (Judges 14:1–3 NASB1995, emphasis added).

When Satan tempted Jesus, he tried to get the Son of God to lust with His eyes, showing the Lord all the kingdoms of the world and offering to give Him everything—without having to endure the cross. Jesus defeated Satan's temptation with the Word of God (Luke 4:8; cf. Deuteronomy 6:13). Jesus would not be swayed by what His eyes saw. He looked past the glories of the world's kingdoms, and "because of the joy awaiting him, he endured the cross, disregarding its shame" (Hebrews 12:2 NLT). In Jesus' case, Satan's appeal to the lust of the eyes fell flat.

The pride of life is another weakness we all succumb to at times. Satan tempts us with the desire to be our own gods, and he is adept at stroking our ego. Eve's desire to be made wise led her to sin in Genesis 3. In her pride of life, she rejected the Lord's right to rule over her and chose instead to make her own decisions. In essence, she became her own god. Christians can play into Satan's hands when they fail to fully surrender to the lordship of Jesus. The pride of life shows itself whenever we give more consideration to pleasing people than to pleasing God. When we say we're open to God's will yet retain "veto power" over His decisions, we are displaying the pride of life.

Satan tempted Jesus with the pride of life in Luke 4:9–11. He gave Jesus an opportunity to "show off" and publicly prove that He was the Son of God. The act would involve a spectacular miracle, the Father's care, and many angels. Jesus' response to Satan's third temptation was to again quote Scripture (Luke 4:12; cf. Deuteronomy 6:16). In "being made in human likeness. . . . he humbled himself" (Philippians 2:7–8). The Lord had no pride to be exploited.

Satan tempts us in many ways, but "we are not unaware of his schemes" (2 Corinthians 2:11). We know he masquerades as an angel of light (2 Corinthians 11:14), trying to make evil look good. We know he manipulates with false guilt, exploits natural weaknesses, and twists Scripture. We know he deceives and distracts and destroys. He has many fiery darts, but they are all quenched with the shield of faith (Ephesians 6:16). We can overcome the temptations of Satan, because "the one who is in you is greater than the one who is in the world" (1 John 4:4).

Satan tempts us through the lust of the flesh, but we "do not live according to the flesh but according to the Spirit" (Romans 8:4). Satan tempts us through the lust of the eyes, but our prayer is, "Turn my eyes away from worthless things; preserve my life according to your word" (Psalm 119:37). Satan tempts us through the pride of life, but we humble ourselves continually before the Lord (1 Peter 5:6; James 4:10).

95. Does a believer have authority over Satan?

The believer's authority over Satan and victory over the spiritual forces of evil depend on the power of God, the relative power of Satan, and God's power within the believer.

First, God's power is perfect and unlimited. He created the heavens and the earth (Genesis 1:1) and holds power over life and death. God clearly has power over Satan and in the end will cast Satan into eternal punishment in the lake of fire (Revelation 20:7–10).

Second, Satan's power, while no match for God's, is yet strong. Satan can tempt humans, as he did with Eve in the Garden of Eden (Genesis 3). He is sometimes granted permission from God to inflict pain on people, as in the case of Job (Job 1–2). He was able to tempt Jesus but unable to cause Him to stumble or sin (Matthew 4:1–11). God warns us that Satan hunts for human victims in the way that a roaring lion prowls for its prey (1 Peter 5:8). Satan's power is not only limited in effectiveness but also in time. Evil faces an ultimate defeat in the future (see Revelation 12:12; 20:10).

This brings us to our power in relation to Satan. Believers in Jesus Christ have God's Spirit living within them. Galatians 2:20 says, "I have been crucified with Christ and I no longer live, but

Christ lives in me." The same power that created the universe resides within us. As a result, Satan has no true power over us. He cannot force us to sin, he cannot possess us, and he knows that we will ultimately have the victory over him.

At the same time, Satan continues to cause problems for believers living in this fallen world. Ephesians 6:10–18 reminds us of the spiritual battle we face and the importance of using the spiritual armor God gives. In addition, James 4:7 spells out our responsibility to resist Satan: "Submit yourselves, then, to God. Resist the devil, and he will flee from you."

We have no authority over Satan in ourselves. God has all authority, and He fights on our behalf. Our response to Satan's attacks should include submitting our lives to God, living in a holy manner, praying for God's protection, and resisting sin. When we place ourselves under God's protection, Satan has no authority over us. He will flee. In addition, we can respond to the devil's temptations as Jesus did. All three times Satan tempted Jesus in the wilderness, the Lord responded by quoting God's Word (Matthew 4:1–11). If Jesus overcame temptation through Scripture, we should certainly rely on the Bible to overcome Satan's temptation in our lives. It's not called the "sword of the Spirit" for nothing (Ephesians 6:17).

The apostle Paul reminds us that Satan's power will be short-lived. Romans 16:20 promises, "The God of peace will soon crush Satan under your feet." Stand firm in the Lord, and you can live in victory over Satan's schemes.

96. What can I do when I am under spiritual attack?

One of the first things to do when we believe we may be under spiritual attack is pray. We should be praying anyway—"without ceasing," according to 1 Thessalonians 5:17 (NKJV)—but our prayers should be that much more intense when we are under attack. God's invitation and promise to Israel can be applied broadly to His children today: "Call upon Me in the day of trouble; I will deliver you, and you shall glorify Me" (Psalm 50:15 NKJV).

When we are under spiritual attack, we must make sure to follow the battle plan of Ephesians 6:10–18. Paul begins with a command to be strong in the Lord and *in His power*—not our own power, which is no match for the devil and his forces. Paul then exhorts us to put on the armor of God, which is the only way to successfully stand against spiritual attacks. In our own strength, we have no chance of defeating the "spiritual forces of evil in the heavenly realms" (Ephesians 6:12). Only the armor of God will equip us properly.

Ephesians 6:13–18 gives a description of the spiritual armor God gives us. Each piece is readily available to all who belong to Christ, because God equips His children. We are to stand firm, buckle on the belt of truth, fasten in place the breastplate of righteousness, wear on our feet the gospel of peace, hold up the shield of faith, wear the helmet of salvation, and wield the sword of the Spirit, which is the Word of God—the only offensive weapon in the whole armory. What do these pieces of spiritual armor represent in spiritual warfare? We are to speak the truth against Satan's lies. We are to rest in the fact that we are declared righteous because of Christ's sacrifice for us. We are to proclaim the gospel no matter how much resistance we receive. We are not to waver in our faith, no matter how fiercely we are attacked. Our ultimate defense is our salvation, of which we are assured. Our weapon is the Word of God, not the word of men and not our own opinions or feelings. Finally, we are to follow Jesus' example "and pray in the Spirit on all occasions with all kinds of prayers and requests" (Ephesians 6:18).

Jesus is our example when it comes to warding off spiritual attacks. Observe how Jesus handled direct attacks from Satan when He was tempted in the wilderness (Matthew 4:1–11). Each temptation was answered the same way—with the words "It is written" and a quote from the Scriptures. Jesus knew the Word of the living God is the most powerful weapon against the temptations of the devil. If Jesus Himself used the Word to counter the devil, do we dare to use anything less?

An example of how *not* to engage in spiritual warfare is the seven sons of Sceva in Ephesus. These men were self-appointed exorcists, and, as they drove out evil spirits, they invoked the name of the Lord Jesus. One day an evil spirit answered them, "'Jesus I know . . . but who are you?' Then the man who had the evil spirit jumped on them and overpowered them all. He gave them such a beating that they ran out of the house naked and bleeding" (Acts 19:15–16). The seven sons of Sceva were using Jesus' name, but they did not have a relationship with Jesus, and their words were void of any power or authority. They stepped into a spiritual battle without the Word of God. As a result, they were humiliated and hurt. May we learn from their bad example and enter the fray with humility, prayer, and the power of the Word.

97. Do Christians have authority to rebuke the devil?

Some Christians believe they not only have the authority to rebuke the devil but are called to be about the business of *continually* rebuking him. There is no biblical basis for such a belief. Satan, unlike God, is not omnipresent. He can only be in one place at a time, and the likelihood of his personally harassing individual Christians is miniscule. Of course, he has legions of demons who do his bidding, and they are everywhere seeking to destroy believers' testimonies. It should be noted here that the Christian cannot be possessed by a demon in the same way people in the Bible are described as being possessed.

As Christians, we are aware of the reality of evil. As we struggle to stand firm in our faith, we realize that our enemies are not merely human ideas but spiritual forces that come from the personal powers of darkness. The Bible says, "For our struggle is not against flesh and blood, but against the rulers, against the authorities, against the powers of this dark world and against the spiritual forces of evil in the heavenly realms" (Ephesians 6:12).

God allows Satan a significant amount of power and influence over the earth, at least for now. Yet Satan is always under God's sovereign control. The Bible tells us that Satan prowls around like a lion in search of prey (1 Peter 5:8). Satan is the power at work in the hearts of those who refuse to obey God (Ephesians 2:2). Those who are not born again by the Holy Spirit of God are under the power of the devil (Acts 26:18; 2 Corinthians 4:4). Christians are no longer enslaved to Satan or to sin (Romans 6:6–7), but this does not mean we are immune to the temptations that he puts before us.

The Bible does not give Christians the authority to rebuke the devil but the power to resist him. James 4:7 says, "Submit yourselves, then, to God. Resist the devil, and he will flee from you." Zechariah 3:2 tells us that it is the Lord who rebukes Satan. Even Michael, one of the most powerful of the holy angels, did not dare accuse Satan, but rather said, "The Lord rebuke you!" (Jude 1:9). In response to Satan's attacks, a Christian should appeal to Christ and trust that the Lord will defeat the forces of evil.

It is not necessary for a Christian to rebuke Satan or to address him in any way. We speak to God, not to demons, because God is the One who must help us. He has already given us His armor (see Ephesians 6:10–18), including the sword of the Spirit, which is the Word of God. When Christ was tempted by Satan, He answered each time with Scripture (see Matthew 4:1–11). The Lord put the sword of the Spirit to good use and left us an example to do the same.

98. What does it mean to give no place to the devil (Ephesians 4:27)?

In Ephesians 4, Paul encourages the believers in Ephesus to live like redeemed Christians. Because they have new life in Christ, they should live like new people, not like they did before they were saved (Ephesians 4:20–24). In the next verses, Paul gives several examples of what it means to live in Christian community. One of those examples involves our anger and the devil. "'Be angry, and do not sin': do not let the sun go down on your wrath, nor give place to the devil" (Ephesians 4:26–27 NKJV). Some translations translate the word for "place" as "foothold" (NIV) or "opportunity" (ESV).

The word for "place" or "foothold" literally refers to a physical location. In the Greek-speaking world, it came to metaphorically mean "opportunity." The sense in Ephesians 4:27 is metaphorical. We are not supposed to give the devil any opportunity to influence our lives. He should not have any place in our lives because he is an enemy of God and wants to destroy God's people (John 8:44; 1 Peter 5:8).

In the context of this passage, it is our anger that has the potential to give the devil an opportunity (Ephesians 4:26). Even righteous anger, if held too long, can lead to bitterness and divisiveness. The longer we remain angry, the more opportunities we are giving the devil to sow hatred and discontentment. That is why Paul tells the Ephesian Christians not to let the sun go down on their anger, so that they do not give the devil any opportunities to twist the situation with his lies and deception. We must dispose of our anger as quickly as possible, so that we do not give any place to the devil.

How do we apply this passage? We must recognize that remaining angry with people gives the devil occasion to wreak havoc in our lives—and anything that gives the devil a chance to influence our lives is bad for us. We should follow Paul's advice, just a few verses later, to be "kind and compassionate to one another, forgiving each other, just as in Christ God forgave you" (Ephesians 4:32).

99. Is it possible to make a deal with the devil?

What if Satan or one of his demons offered you a deal: He will give you anything your heart desires—wealth, power, beauty, great skill, etc. In exchange, he owns your soul for all eternity.

The idea of making a deal with the devil was explored in the classic legend of Faust, a scholar who made a bargain with a demon named Mephistopheles. Many similar stories have been told around the same theme. In some of the legends, the person tricks the devil in some way, escaping the contract and getting his soul back. In others, the devil wins with deception or a double-cross.

In any case, the idea of forfeiting one's soul in a deal with the devil is much more cultural and literary than it is biblical. The Bible never records an account of a human being bargaining with Satan or demons.

The Bible does depict the devil as a dealmaker, of sorts. In the book of Genesis, for instance, the serpent promises Eve good things: "Your eyes will be opened," he says, "and you will be like God" (Genesis 3:5). All Eve has to do is take the fruit that she can easily see is "good for food and pleasing to the eye" (Genesis 3:6). It was a trick, of course, and Eve suffered the consequence of her sinful choice (v. 16). Satan got what he wanted—or so it seemed. He also received a curse in the end (vv. 14–15).

When Jesus Christ was beginning His public ministry, the devil attempted to make a deal with Him. In exchange for the Lord's worship, the devil offered Jesus "all the kingdoms of the world and their splendor" (Matthew 4:8). Jesus sends Satan away with a rebuke from God's Word (v. 10).

The Bible gives no support to the notion that people can make a deal with the devil, but some people have attempted to make such a bargain unilaterally, pledging themselves to Satan in hopes of receiving some special favors from him. In a sense, that's the nature of idolatry and witchcraft as described in the Bible. When a pagan worshiper dedicated a sacrifice to his gods, he hoped for something in return—fruitful crops, victory in battle, etc. (see 2 Chronicles 28:23). When a sorcerer or witch practiced her craft, she attempted to complete a transaction, hoping to gain special knowledge, power, or control.

From the Bible's perspective, even if it were possible to make a deal with the devil, doing so would be unwise for several reasons:

- The Bible reveals Satan to be a liar. He is adept at deception and duplicity. Jesus condemned Satan as "the father of lies" (John 8:44). The devil takes what is true and twists it to corrupt and destroy human beings. Anyone who would attempt to deal with such a being is a fool.
- While Satan has some measure of authority as the "prince of the power of the air" (Ephesians 2:2 ESV), his power is not absolute—only God has absolute power. Also, the pleasures of sin endure only "for a season" (Hebrews 11:25 KJV), and any theoretical pact made with Satan would end in misery. He is a thief whose goal is "to steal and kill and destroy" (see John 10:10).
- Satan cannot own human souls. All souls belong to the God who created them (Ezekiel 18:4). Hell is not Satan's kingdom. Despite all the jokes and stories to the contrary, Satan will not reign as master of hell, relishing his power over human souls; no, he will be sentenced to the lake of fire as a prisoner himself (Revelation 20:10).

The truth is far worse than the legend of Faust would imply. According to God's Word, every human soul is already bound for hell. No deal with the devil need be struck to ensure that fate. Because of our sin, we are "by nature deserving of wrath" (Ephesians 2:3). We stand "condemned already" (John 3:18). Apart from a change of course, our souls will end up in hell without ever having to trade them away to Satan.

We don't need a deal with the devil—we're already on his side—we need a deal with *God*. We need Him to save our souls, to change our destination. The problem is that we have nothing to offer Him in trade. He needs nothing from us (Romans 11:33–36), and all our attempts to appease His wrath through religious observance are futile (Isaiah 1:11). But the good news—the gospel—is that God loves us and has offered us a unilateral "bargain" of His own: He will save our souls, giving us everything our hearts truly desire for eternity, in exchange for nothing but our faith in His Son, Jesus Christ. In a great exchange, Jesus has appeased God's wrath for us, taking our sin and its penalty upon Himself (1 John 4:10; 1 Peter 2:24). In Christ, God will make us alive when we were dead. He will fill our futile lives on this side of eternity with meaningful work and joyful anticipation. See Ephesians 2:1–10 to read more about this pact that God offers.

100. Why is "the devil made me do it" not a valid excuse?

The first instance of "the devil made me do it" used as an excuse was in the Garden of Eden. Eve says, "The serpent deceived me, and I ate" (Genesis 3:13). Her excuse did not get her off the hook (v. 16), and it won't help us much, either.

Yes, the devil and his demons tempt us to sin (Genesis 3; Luke 4; 1 Peter 5:8). But "the devil made me do it" is far too often used to excuse our own bad choices. Except in an instance of demon possession, the devil cannot *make* us do anything. The devil is absolutely worthy of blame for much of the evil in the world, but using the devil as a scapegoat for our own sinful choices is counterproductive to achieving victory over sin.

Demon possession is a condition in which a demon or demons inhabit a person and have complete control over that person (see Mark 9:22). Christians cannot be demon possessed. The indwelling Holy Spirit will not allow it (Romans 8:9; Ephesians 5:18). Therefore, the devil and his demons cannot control a believer. They cannot make us do anything involuntarily. So, rather than blame the devil for our sin, we need to look at ourselves.

James 1:14 declares, "Each person is tempted when he is lured and enticed by his *own* desire" (ESV, emphasis added). Why do we sin? We sin because we are sinners. We are plagued by and infected with sin (Romans 3:10–23). While demonic oppression and influence are real, the primary problem is our sinful nature. "Now the works of the flesh are evident: sexual immorality, impurity, sensuality, idolatry, sorcery, enmity, strife, jealousy, fits of anger, rivalries, dissensions, divisions, envy, drunkenness, orgies, and things like these" (Galatians 5:19–21 ESV). Notice, it's the "works of the flesh" in this list, not the works of the devil.

As Christians, we have the indwelling Holy Spirit to help us overcome sin (1 John 4:4). We have everything we need for life and godliness (2 Peter 1:3). If we sin, we have no excuse. We cannot blame the devil. We cannot blame our circumstances. We can only blame ourselves. And, until we recognize that the problem resides within us (Romans 7:20), we will never arrive at the solution.

It may sound harsh to tell someone that the problem is himself and his own choices. But it's no harsher than a doctor telling a patient to quit smoking and that the tobacco company is not to blame for his poor health. To find a cure, one must start with a correct diagnosis and then move to the correct treatment. The correct diagnosis is sin. The treatment is to submit to God and obey His Word. God can enable us to achieve victory over sin (Romans 7:24–25; 1 John 5:3–5).

If you are a Christian and you commit a sin, the devil did not make you do it. He may have tempted you to do it. He may have influenced you and even set you up with a tantalizing opportunity. But he did not *make* you do it. You still had a choice. God never allows you to be tempted beyond your ability to withstand, and He always provides a way of escape (1 Corinthians 10:13). A Christian saying, "The devil made me do it," denies the truth of 1 John 4:4: "Little children, you are from God and have overcome them, for he who is in you is greater than he who is in the world" (ESV).

Notes

Section 1 Questions About the Spiritual Realm

1. Thomas Ken, "Praise God from Whom All Blessings Flow" (1674), https://hymnary.org/text/praise_god_from_whom_all_blessings_ken.

Section 4 Questions About Types of Angels

1. This nine-level hierarchy was proposed by Pseudo-Dionysius the Areopagite, a theologian and philosopher of the late fifth to early sixth centuries, in *Di Coelesti Hierarchia (The Celestial Hierarchy)* and further explored by St. Thomas Aquinas in *Summa Theologica* 1.108.1–8.
2. "Isaiah—Vision and Service—A Seraph's Wings," in *MacLaren's Expositions*, under "Isaiah 6:2," Bible Hub, accessed March 25, 2026, https://biblehub.com/commentaries/isaiah/6-2.htm.
3. "Theological Significance," in *Topical Encyclopedia*, under "Watcher," Bible Hub, accessed March 25, 2026, https://biblehub.com/topical/w/watcher.htm.
4. See Origen, *Homilies on Luke,* homily 12.

Section 7 Questions About the Nephilim

1. Guiness World Records, "Robert Wadlow: Tallest Man Ever," accessed March 16, 2026, https://www.guinnessworldrecords.com/records/hall-of-fame/robert-wadlow-tallest-man-ever.

Section 8 Questions About Types of Demons

1. Geza Vermes, trans., *The Complete Dead Sea Scrolls in English,* rev. ed. (Penguin, 2011), 417.

Section 9 Questions About Satan

1. John Milton, *Paradise Lost,* bk. 1, lines 261–263.
2. Martin Luther, "A Mighty Fortress Is Our God," 1529, trans. Frederic Hedge.

3. "End of the Trial: Guardian Report on the Executions, 16 October 1946," *Manchester Guardian*, October 7, 1946, in "Final Moments of Nazis Executed at Nuremburg," *The Guardian*, September 11, 2009, https://www.theguardian.com/world/2009/sep/11/nazis-nuremberg-executed-hermann-goring.

Section 10 Questions About Satan's Abilities

1. Fr. Mario Attard, "The Message of Our Lady of Guadalupe," *Catholic Journal*, December 19, 2024, https://catholicjournal.us/2024/12/19/the-message-of-our-lady-of-guadalupe/.

2. Thomas Griffin, "The Three Commands of Fatima: Love Her Heart, Save Souls, Pray for Peace," *National Catholic Register*, May 13, 2025, https://www.ncregister.com/blog/griffin-fatima-three-words.

3. Andrew Cesanek, "Mary IS Co-Redemptrix and Mediatrix of All Graces," The Fatima Center, November 7, 2025, https://fatima.org/news-views/immaculate-heart-of-mary/.

4. Frère Michel de la Sante Trinité, *The Whole Truth About Fatima*, vol. 2, 497–500, quoted in "Fatima: A Call for Reparation," The Fatima Center, January 20, 2026, https://fatima.org/news-views/cr-135/fatima-a-call-for-reparation/.

5. "The Apparitions and the Miraculous Medal," Chapelle Notre-Dame de la Médaille Miraculeuse, accessed April 5, 2026, https://www.chapellenotredamedelamedaillemiraculeuse.com/langues/english/apparitions-et-la-medaille-miraculeuse-gb/.

Section 11 Questions About Us and Demons

1. "Matthew Poole's Commentary," Matthew 12, Bible Hub, accessed April 5, 2026, https://biblehub.com/commentaries/poole/matthew/12.htm.

Acknowledgments

A special thanks goes out to Kevin Stone and Athalia Bufano, who spent countless hours compiling, editing, and proofreading the answers that went into this book. I'd also like to thank the staff of Got Questions Ministries. Without their hard work, commitment, and passion, this ministry would not be possible. Thank you, also, to the more than eight hundred individuals who have served as volunteer question answerers for GotQuestions.org in the past twenty-four years. GotQuestions.org never has been, and will never be, a one-man show. Above all, to God be the glory—great things He has done (Romans 11:36)!

Shea Michael Houdmann is the president, CEO, and founder of Got Questions Ministries, the parent organization of GotQuestions.org, one of the most frequently visited Christian websites in the world, with over 2.6 billion pageviews in twenty-four years. With GotQuestions.org having received over one million questions submitted from people around the world, Shea has tremendous insights into the questions people are actually asking. He has earned a master of arts in Christian theology from Calvary Theological Seminary and a master of theology with an emphasis in apologetics from Dallas Theological Seminary. He is also currently pursuing a doctor of ministry degree from Dallas Theological Seminary. Shea and his wife, MeLissa, have been married for twenty-nine years. In his limited free time, Shea loves dating his wife, watching and playing sports, hiking, off-roading, movies, and hanging out with his German shepherd.

NOTES

NOTES

NOTES

NOTES

NOTES